Please Note: This ebook is formatted so that it can be read on any e-reading device, including smartphones. As different devices have different dimensions, page numbers will vary - hence this document does not contain formatted page numbers. Those numbers on the Table of Contents are a guide on desktops & laptops only.

?

Introduction by Nicola Cairncross

Why did I re-write this classic book "The Science Of Getting Rich" and adapt it for the internet age?

After 20 years of making a full time living online, but watching others try and fail, I have been constantly fascinated by what makes the difference between those who make it and those who don't?

Is it the tools or tactics they are using? Are there some secrets that only those in the "Inner Circles" know and don't share? Is it the kind of traffic they use?

Having read this classic book (original version by Wallace D. Wattles) right at the beginning of my online journey back in 1998, I really didn't "get it". But now, after 20 years, when I read it again I realised all the secrets to online success were in here all the time!

However, the archaic nature of the language, examples and references made it impenetrable for the modern online entrepreneur.

So my mission to re-write this old classic and make it easier to read and understand started...

Still I hesitated to do it, for sure, I couldn't believe someone hadn't already done it.

When the idea came to me, I wrestled with the idea, it seemed so right but who was I to do it? Surely someone more successful should step up?

But the longer I thought about it, the more pressing the need to take it on as a project became. When I really thought about it, I had several good reasons for it to be me.

Why Me?

I have failed for years, always seeking to "better myself" as it was called when I was growing up, but not having a clue how to go about that. Then I succeeded big and failed big, then succeeded again.

Because we are not taught this stuff in schools. The school system was created (and is still run today) to churn out good little workers for the benefit of the multi-corporations and the wealthy. As you will see later, if we all became rich, who would run things? Who would work in the hotels and restaurants, who would fly the planes, who would make the cars, who would build the houses?

I'm not upset or cross about that, by the way, thinking about the daft education we got. It's just how things are at the moment (although the move to home schooling is encouraging) and if you come from parents who don't think about it, and you don't have any mentor in your life who can show you a better way, you'll struggle to become more successful, just like I did.

I was clueless about success and money until the age of 38, when I had two small children, my husband had just been made redundant for the third time and I was going around the recruitment consultants trying to get a secretarial job at £12,000 a year (around $15,000) .

I knew I was worth better than that, after all I was bright and hard working, I'd started and run companies, one of which, our record label Esoteric Records, had had some minor critical success but never made any money.

I came to the realisation one day in a garden in Kensal Road, London, that no prince was coming to save me, that I needed to take 100% responsibility for my own success and the well being of my family.

As you'll discover in this book, as soon as I made that decision and, more importantly, started to take action on it, things started to change for the better.

I landed a dream job with an inspirational mentor – entrepreneur & philanthropist Bennie Gray of the Space Organisation in London, within just a couple of weeks.

Then, when working for Bennie, I literally fell over a little book in Books Etc Oxford St, London that showed me (after about 7 re-reads) how to become financially free, a concept I'd never heard of before.

That book was "Swimming With Piranha Makes You Hungry" by Professor Colin Turner – little did I know I would interview him 10 years later and he would give me 200 of their books for my students!

And so I embarked on a journey of personal development starting with reading the life-changing book "7 Habits Of Highly Effective People" by Steven Covey.

(I'll be mentioning quite a few life-changing books throughout this book, but don't worry about making a note of them now, here's a link to my "Top 30 Books of All Time").

Within the next 5 years, I was to land a second dream job, move back to my home town by the seaside then, buy, live in and renovate a 7 bedroom house with my husband, kids, sister, brother in law and their kids, then buy, renovate, launch, run and then sell, a 12 bedroom hotel "no money down".

I also launched a coaching business called The Money Gym, wrote a book of the same name and build that into a 3-partner, 5 x coaches and six figure business.

All of that, working from home, bringing up my kids and being there for them whenever they needed me.

Then the recession hit, along with a global credit crunch and on the 11th January 2010, I lost everything.

Long story, but it hit me hard. For two years, I lived in my sister's spare room, my kids had to go and live with their Dad, as I couldn't put a roof over my head, let alone theirs.

I couldn't give my expertise in online marketing and wealth creation away. I used to go to my local Chamber of Commerce and sit on their website committee for free in the hope of someone, anyone would ask me to help them with their marketing.

Nobody did.

But within 5 years of that fateful day in January, 2010, I was back with another six-figure turnover business, ClicksAndLeads.com, a boutique Social Media PPC agency, and this time, once I made my mind up to launch that business in late 2014, I'd done it in under 6 months (would have been 3 but a friend was sick and I had to spend a lot of time in hospital with him).

So what made the difference? What was it that made me wallow in poverty from 2010 to the end of 2014 then come back with a bang within 6 months?

I'm going to reveal all in this book by Wallace D. Wattles, lovingly rewritten by me, for you.

Because the first time I read "The Science Of Getting Rich", back in 2003 or 2004, along with the more famous book that followed it "Think And Grow Rich" by Napoleon Hill, I just didn't get it.

Those books laid it all out for me – the most important information in the whole world was there for me to know - but I just couldn't absorb the information in the way it was presented.

The book was totally male orientated, written in archaic language, loads of references to religion and God (who, being a confirmed agnostic then, I just didn't believe in) and somehow all those things combined to make sure I just didn't' get it.

At the time I was looking for surefire tactics to implement and not esoteric, waffly thoughts from some old school geezer back in the day!

The only reason I re-read the book was because my podcast co-host Judith Morgan and I had just interviewed Jacqueline Rogers, founder of The Athena Network for our "Beyond The Laptop Lifestyle" virtual summit. Judith needed some time off, we needed some co-presenters, Jacqueline had been a big hit on the Summit so we knew she was right for the podcast too.

We have a section on the podcast called "Project Updates" and she told me in that section that, as it was out of copyright, she was re-writing "The Science Of Getting Rich" for women and I was struck by what a great idea that was.

I went off and found a copy online, printed it off and read it through again and as I did I found that (religious references notwithstanding) I agreed with every single word! It all made total sense based on what I had been through in the last 5 years and I just got it.

How A Book & A Science Show Changed My Thinking

A while ago, I read a book called "Synchronicity: The Inner Path Of Leadership" by Joseph Jaworski.

From Amazon: Synchronicity is an inspirational guide to developing the most essential leadership capacity for our time: the ability to collectively shape our future. By telling the story of their remarkable journey toward an understanding of the deep issues of leadership, Joseph Jaworski explains the fundamental shifts of mind that will enable leaders to listen to realities that want to emerge in this world and acquire the courage to personify them.

The reason I loved it particularly, was it told Joseph's own "Hero's Journey" story of having a nervous breakdown, then travelling the world in search of a new life, but some co-incidences lead him to study the phenomenon of Synchronicity, talking to many physicists along the way, and how that can be partially, if not completely be explained by Quantum Physics.

More recently, I watched the short series on British TV called "The Forces Of Nature" presented by Professor Brian Cox.

Brian Edward Cox, OBE FRS is an English physicist, and Advanced Fellow of particle physics in the School of Physics and Astronomy at the University of Manchester. Perhaps he was one of the people Joseph Jaworski talked to when writing their book?

Cox has been described as the natural successor for leading the BBC's scientific programming by both David Attenborough and the late Patrick Moore and I have to agree – he makes the most complicated concepts almost completely understandable.

(Amusingly, before their academic career, Cox was a keyboard player for the band D:Ream, best known for their hit "Things Will Only Get Better" a positive upbeat song if ever I heard one!)

From the description of the series on the BBC website:

"Professor Brian Cox combines some of the most spectacular sights on Earth with our deepest understanding of the universe to reveal how the planet's beauty is created by just a handful of forces".

The science is amazing, the photography / filming is amazing, the music is amazing and he blew my mind with some of the statements he made, one while walking through an English ancient woodland, holding up an acorn.

"Life is just the temporary home of the immortal elements that build up the Universe"

Nice!

He went on to explain the Time / Space continuum, which he explained by pointing out that we are hurtling through space at around 650 miles an hour, even though when we stand on the surface of the planet it doesn't feel like we are moving at all.

He talked about how that planet was also moving around the Sun as well as rotating on it's axis and somehow, all that meant that there was a Time / Space Continuum which itself meant somehow that everything that happens to us – good or bad - is happening still out there in the Universe somewhere, that every moment still exists and every moment that will exist, already exists.

This could even mean that there are an infinite number of Universes (the "Many Worlds" theory) existing right next to each other.

Mind officially blown now!

Later in the same show he said "We are of the Earth, constructed from a ready supply of chemical elements, forged in the Stars"

I've been thinking about energy, specifically life energy a lot recently as I just lost my best friend (and life partner) Steve Watson, who died very suddenly back in March 2016, just a few months ago as I write this. I'm over the worst of the grieving, the agonising minute by minute pain that you feel in the early days, the many unanswerable questions are subsiding and I just get very, very sad sometimes at what we'll miss out on for the rest of the time we would have had together. But I've also been finding the psychology of grieving very interesting and I'm sure that's why I'm feeling better sooner than I ever thought I would, especially in the early days.

I found Prof. Cox's words very moving and somewhat consoling in my loss. The thought that every wonderful moment we had (and all the fights!) are still happening out there somewhere, made it all feel a bit less final.

However, the bigger concept for the purposes of explaining one of the reasons why I wanted to rewrite this book for you, was the concept that we were all made of the same stuff, not just us humans, but the acorn he was holding, the fallen tree Prof. Cox was sitting on, the sofa I was sitting on, the TV I was watching him on...

We are all made from a mixture of a fewer number of exactly 92 chemical elements, forged in the stars, by some miracle of evolution and that we are on earth for a tiny, tiny amount of time...well, when I read "The Science Of Getting Rich" again, it all just suddenly clicked into place.

Remember, Prof Cox said "Life is just the temporary home of the immortal elements that build up the Universe"

Life itself, that ephemeral thing, that can't be bottled or hung onto, but can be seen and enjoyed and be seen to leave, that's the miracle I can get my arms around.

For all we know, there could be other stuff – not just animals – out there, which thinks.

We know so little yet of how the human mind works, what creates and fuels the thing we call the soul.

"We have no idea how widespread "intelligence" is in the cosmos. From our present knowledge, the most complex things in the Universe are ourselves, in particular, our brains. What's remarkable is that atoms have assembled into entities which are somehow able to ponder their origins" Sir Martin Rees, British cosmologist and astrophysicist, from the video "What We Still Don't Know: Are We Real?"

Part 2 of the same video series asserts "Everything you thought you knew about the universe is wrong. It's made of atoms, right? Wrong. Atoms only account for a measly 15% of everything that exists. The mass of the universe consists of something so mysterious and elusive that it has been dubbed 'dark matter'".

Writing this in 2016, I have to wonder how Wallace D. Wattles could have possibly imagined things that are only just starting to be proved now?

Nowadays I'm a confirmed atheist, preferring the total liberation that comes when you know, deep in your heart, that nothing outside you has any dominion over what happens to you, that there is no ethereal deity who could come and save you but chooses not to, that whatever happens for good or ill, it's all down to you as to how you react to it.

But I do believe in things like Mediation and how it can change the way you think, feel and act. Here's a quote from a great article by Vishen from Mindvalley where he got hooked up to a brain scanner that can actually measure what goes on when you meditate.

"Having collected a vast amount of data, they discovered that different brainwave patterns were associated to different types of people. They studied highly creative people, Zen monks, billionaires. All of them showed very different and distinct brainwave patterns.

But what's really exciting was that he found a way to train people to replicate these patterns....it's not just alpha waves which are important. There are other waves discovered, that correlate to different experiences. Theta waves for example, correlate with flashes of creativity and intuition. And Delta waves are, in their words, associated to "altering reality."

Interestingly, even though my alpha waves weren't nearly as high as some of the other creative minds in the group, I scored much higher delta wave production. And according to our trainers at the program, this is only seen in less than 1% of the population. Following the time in the chamber we'd then meet with trainers at the institute who would look over our brain scans and help us understand what exactly was going on in our minds".

So, with quantum physics and even studies of the changes in electrical activity in the brain of creative people and billionaires starting to look like they are backing up Wallace's theories, let's go back to the book....

If you change the words Wallace used, it all makes sense in the 21st Century too.

If you change the word "God" into "Universal Energy", if you change the words "Formless Stuff" (which distracted me so horribly on my first reading, from the message contained in the book by making me think of see-through jelly), into "Building Blocks Of Life", shorthand for those 92 odd chemical elements, the atoms and "dark matter" between them, and if you change the words "Increasing" into "Abundance", it all suddenly makes sense to this 54 year old, feminist, atheist, digital marketer.

"Our experience teaches us that there are indeed laws of nature, regularities in the way things behave, and that these laws are best expressed using the language of mathematics. This raises the interesting possibility that mathematical consistency might be used to guide us, along with experimental observation, to the laws that describe physical reality, and this has proved to be the case time and again throughout the history of science....and it is truly one of the wonderful mysteries of our universe that it should be so." Brian Cox, Why Does $E=mc^2$?

Why "The Science Of Getting Rich Online"?

Well, I've made my living online for the last 20 years. I know that getting rich online is a science and it's not a very complicated one.

It involves solving a problem and then putting a compelling and value driven offer in front of as large a number of people as possible.

In fact, it was in the book "Think & Grow Rich" by Napoleon Hill that I read the words, in the dining room of the house we were doing up, in 1999...

"If you can find the biggest numbers of people to serve, the rivers of abundance will flow for you". I think it went on to say that they would flow faster and stronger than you can ever imagine, but I'd have to re-read the book to be sure.

And I thought, "He means the internet! That's where the biggest numbers of people to serve are, right now".

There are a number of tools that you can use, to make it easier and those tools are quite intuitive to use, and come with great tuition videos to help you learn how to use them.

I've created and launched 3 books online (this is the 4th and I've got at least one more in me). I've launched two podcasts and still co-host "Own It! Your Business & Your Life" and I've started many online businesses, two reaching a six-figure turnover.

However, as is the way of things, about 95% of people who try to achieve the goal of becoming rich online will fail.

Unlike me, who succeeded then failed spectacularly, then succeeded again, these people fail before they even get going.

And, after 20+ years making a full time living online, as someone who was using computers before Windows, who made her first website using cold hard HTML code, who remembers a time before Facebook, Youtube and Twitter let alone Instagram, Snapchat and Musical.ly, I've become increasingly fascinated with that fact.

I've seen so many people fail online it's not funny.

I've also seen many people succeed online and succeed big. Bigger than me.

When you hit a home run online, it's enormous. I have personally met people who make upwards of $50,000 a month selling native made bracelets from Bali on Amazon. I've met people making that same kind of money from selling other people's information products. I've been mentored by people who charge between $10,000 and $100,000 a day for their time, expertise and knowledge.

I'm not going to quote numbers at you (because they'll be out of date before I hit "save"). The online population is growing exponentially and they are hungry for products, services and information. They are also willing to pay for all three. The days of the internet being free are long gone.

The most valuable thing of all now in most people's lives is time and they are more than willing to pay for it, or even the illusion of it (Uber being a great example).

What makes the difference between the ones who succeed online and the ones who fail? What makes the difference between the people who make a lovely living online and live the life they always wanted.

I'm going to tell you straight, don't you worry.

This book is down to earth and direct. It is intended for everyone who wants to discover how to make money online but who want to be ethical about it and use only legitimate means – those means not being either spammy or scammy.

It's intended for people who want to sell solutions and services to solve problems, or to help those with expertise, knowledge, passions, hobbies, and interests of all kinds.

It is for those who have bought course after course, paid guru after so-called guru and who have finally started to realise that there is no "magic button" or "silver bullet" that will make them rich overnight.

It's for those who are now willing to take consistent action day after day, moving forward in the knowledge that one day, their small, consistent actions will bear fruit and create a great living – or even riches - online.

I'm going to expect you to listen and act, knowing that the knowledge I'm sharing with you in homage to the late Wallace D. Wattles, is real, it works and I've proved it works by earning my full time living by working online for the last 20 years.

The Science of Getting Rich was one of the first books I read, right at the beginning of my entrepreneurial career, that even hinted at the "Law Of Attraction".

While I went on to read the other books on this topic, such as "The Alchemist" by Paulo Coelho, "Think & Grow Rich" by Napoleon Hill and to watch the movie "The Secret", I largely missed the point of all of them, as they didn't contain instructions – there was no step by step "how to" included at all. They kept hinting at the "secret of success" contained within but nowhere was it spelled out so it became blindingly bleeding obvious.

So, having missed that secret hidden in plain sight apparently, I kept looking for the perfect online business plan, the best, most up to date strategy, tactic or tool.

If it was 100% down to that course of action, truthfully, every person who does exactly as their guru tells them should certainly get rich; for the science herein applied is an exact science, and, if someone has succeeded using that guru's method before, then surely, failure for you is impossible?

I'm going to mention certain tried and tested methods of making money online, or tactics and tools – but never tricks - to help with the same, and I'll give credit to the creators or engineers of those freely, as the tapestry of tools at our disposal are many and varied but, over time, one tool or tactic usually wins out as being the best.

Each element of internet marketing (or digital marketing as it's more often called now) has usually built on another element that went before, for nowhere else is the "standing on the shoulders of giants" more prevalent than online.

I'm doing it myself right now, by re-writing this classic book, 100% legally as it's now out of copyright (now that was a serious oversight by somebody somewhere!).

Interestingly, with the internet has come the increasing acceptance that copyright is obsolete and I'm never happier than when someone quotes from one of my books or blog posts, as long as they mention my name and link back to my website of course!

Why did I want to rewrite this book and position it to help those who want to become experts in internet marketing, digital marketing or those who simply want to create a second income online, next to that earned from their "day job"?

Because I've seen so many people fail at the very thing I've earned my living from for over 20 years now, bringing up two children pretty much as a single mother for over 10 of those.

Why do they fail, when the science of making money online is so simple?

Because they haven't got their heads straight.

My two kids Phoebe & Nelson – now young adults really – are not academic at all but they are also not carrying around any emotional baggage.

They don't have major self esteem issues that some of the bigger life knocks can give you – if you don't have a firm grip on your mind and the rantings of your ego voice by then.

When young people decide they want something, they don't generally have so many voices inside their head telling them all the reasons why they can't do it.

(Oh! Just one voice you say? Only me that has several voices then....let's keep that between us).

At the moment, I'm teaching my son Nelson how to promote himself better online.

He is an aspiring DJ and music producer (his working name is DJ Nelzen) he's producing their own house, garage and grime music (don't ask, I haven't figured out what grime is yet and I used to work in the music industry!) You can check him out on Soundcloud and Facebook.

I'm also helping my highly creative daughter, Phoebe who studied beauty (but doesn't want to be a beautician) and who loves makeup, fashion, travel and popular culture, but who is very, very definite that she doesn't want to continue working for just over minimum wage at our local gastropub.

She is studying harder than she ever did at school, to become a better YouTube and Instagram marketer. She may even be offering those services to others by the time you read this.

But I also spend a bit of time with someone else, younger than me but older than my kids who, despite having a great online business idea and being highly skilled at all the elements needed to bring that business idea to fruition, just seems to be completely incapable of taking any action.

Why that is, what causes that block, is not a lack of strategy, not a lack of tactics or tools, perhaps it's just simply down to how they feel about themselves and what that means in terms of being able to move forwards.

Perhaps you are struggling with the same issues?

Well, all that can be changed by reading and applying the practices in this book, which I've endeavoured to bring bang up to date for the 21st Century and make accessible to you today.

For Those Who Also Want Step By Step Tactics!

I've also included a list of how I would start an online business, with my preferred tools to use as I'm writing this book now.

There are links at the end of the book to my "Perfect Online Business Plan" which is a perfect step by step Blueprint for experts, authors and consultants to start taking their business online.

Please DO NOT skip to those links without reading this book first. It's not tools, techniques or tactics remember, that makes the difference between success or failure online.

It's what goes on between your ears!

I want you to be able to read this book, start to dream big, take massive action and THEN get started with the practical elements of "The Science Of Getting Rich Online"

Come and tell me how you get on at NicolaCairncross.com?

Nicola Cairncross
August 2016

The Right to Be Rich

"The Best Way To Predict Your Future Is To Create It" Abraham Lincoln

WHATEVER may be said in praise of poverty, the fact remains that it is not possible to live a really complete or successful life unless you are rich, that is that you have a large surplus of money, beyond that amount you need to live on a day to day, month by month, year by year basis.

No person can rise to their greatest potential unless they have plenty of money; for to find the greatest fulfilment in life you must have many things to use, and you cannot have these things unless you have the money to buy them with.

While the recent rise of minimalism is advocating the use of less things in our day to day lives, we all still need a certain number of things in our life, to make it safe, comfortable and fun. You can decide how many or how few things you want in your life, but wouldn't it be great if all of them were of the best quality possible?

A person develops in mind, soul, and body by not being worried about money on a day to day basis, and by making use of great quality things, and society is organised so that person must have money in order to become the possessor of great quality things; therefore, the basis of all advancement for a person must be the science of getting rich.

The object of all life is development; and everything that lives has an right to all the fullest development of life it is capable of attaining.

A person's right to life means their right to have the free and unrestricted use of all the things which may be necessary to their fullest mental, spiritual, and physical potential; or, in other words, their right to be rich.

In this book, I shall not speak of riches in a figurative way; to be really rich does not mean just to be satisfied or contented with a little.

No person ought to be satisfied with little if he is capable of using and enjoying more.

The purpose of Nature is the advancement and full development of the full potential of life; and every person should have all that can contribute to the power; elegance, beauty, and richness of life; to be content with less goes against the very nature of the life force within us.

The person who owns all he wants, for the living of all the life he is capable of living, is rich; and the simple truth is that no person who has not got plenty of money can have all he wants.

Life has advanced so far, and become so complex, that even the most ordinary person requires what, in previous times would be a great amount of wealth in order to live in a manner that even approaches completeness.

Every person naturally wants to become all that they are capable of becoming; this desire to realise innate possibilities is inherent in human nature; we cannot help wanting to be all that we can be.

Success in life is becoming what you want to be; you can become what you want to be only by making use of things, and you can have the free use of things only as you become rich enough to buy them. To understand the science of getting rich is therefore the most essential of all knowledge.

There is nothing wrong in wanting to get rich. The desire for riches is really the desire for a richer, fuller, and more abundant life; and that desire is praise worthy.

There are three motives for which we live; we live for the body, we live for the mind, we live for the soul.

No one of these is better or holier than the other; all are alike desirable, and no one of the three-- body, mind, or soul--can live fully if either of the others is cut short of full life and expression. It is not right or noble to live only for the soul and deny mind or body; and it is wrong to live for the intellect and deny body or soul.

We are all acquainted with the loathsome consequences of living for the body and denying both mind and soul; and we see that real life means the complete expression of all that person can give forth through body, mind, and soul.

Drug addicts, alcoholics and even those people who push their body to the limits in competitions while abusing steroids are living wholly for the body and not for mind or soul.

Whatever you say, no person can be really happy or satisfied unless their body is living fully in every function, and unless the same is true of your mind and soul.

Wherever there is unexpressed possibility, or function not performed, there is unsatisfied desire. Desire is possibility seeking expression, or function seeking performance.

You cannot live fully in body without good food, comfortable clothing, and warm shelter; and without freedom from excessive toil. Rest and recreation are also necessary to your physical life.

You cannot live fully in mind without books and time to study them, without opportunity for travel and observation, or without intellectual companionship.

To live fully in mind you must have intellectually stimulating pastimes, and you must surround yourself with all the objects of music, art and beauty you are capable of using and appreciating.

To live fully in soul, you must have companionship and love; and love is denied expression by poverty. Just look at the statistics for divorce and the reasons given for those divorces if you don't believe me.

Your highest happiness is found in the bestowal of benefits on those you love; love finds its most natural and spontaneous expression in giving and we are not just talking about emotionally giving. Presents and holidays and the ability to have time to just be together in beautiful and nurturing surroundings without money worries, all help a lot.

The person who has nothing to contribute cannot fill their place as a family member, as a citizen, or as a person. It is in the use of material things to nurture their family and pursue their passions and interests that a person finds full life for their body, develops their mind, and unfolds their soul.

It is therefore of supreme importance to you that you should become rich. It is perfectly right that you should desire to be rich; if you are a normal person you cannot help doing so.

It is perfectly right that you should give your best attention to the Science of Getting Rich, for it is the noblest and most necessary of all studies. If you neglect this study, you are derelict in your duty to yourself, to Universal Energy and humanity; for you can render to Universal Energy and humanity no greater service than to make the most of yourself

As Daniel Priestley so eloquently spells out in his book, "Entrepreneur Revolution", the Industrial Revolution, with its long working day and school system designed to turn out good little factory workers, is a relatively recent construct.

Before the Industrial Revolution, most people did work that played to their strengths, work that was both in demand and they were good at. You learned from the best, who were always looking for the next generation to pass their skills onto. You wouldn't have been apprenticed to the best baker in town if your skill was in making swords or creating amazing head gear!

This had a multi-benefit effect; the things that you are good at, you often really enjoy doing, if you really enjoy doing something you tend to do it faster so produce more and you produce higher quality goods or services so you can command better prices and make more money doing it.

You get a huge sense of satisfaction from being good at something, your day to day work is meaningful because others appreciate your output and you have a sense of control, because nobody can suddenly say to you "stop doing that" – why would they? Even if you had to move suddenly to another location, often simple tools would enable you to get up and running again in no time.

Roll on 100 years and the Cubicle, where people work within a corporate environment, is a square, grey prison, surrounded by many other identical cubicles, within a room where only the very lucky (or, more often the very senior) get a glimpse of natural daylight.

In the Northern Hemisphere, many millions of people get up in the dark, go to work in the dark, take their lunch break (if they get one) in artificial light (because it takes too long to get out of the building) and then go home in the dark.

And it's making us not only miserable but sick.

Apart from the self medication that goes on, from overeating to drinking too much, digital addictions like playing hours of World Of Warcraft or Call Of Duty, or the use of recreational drugs, stress causes all kinds of horrible diseases and the thing that causes humans the most stress is not feeling in control of your own life and well being

Everyone is terrified of losing their job because if you can't work, you can't provide for yourself or your family. You can lose your job at a moment's notice, due to external circumstances that are nothing to do with your skill at your job.

The only way to create financial security and alleviate the danger if you work in corporate life is to increase the gap between what you earn and what you spend and invest the difference in "income producing assets" that may eventually create financial freedom at the point where the income from those assets cover your living expenses.

Even then, if you invest that money in anything but your own business, you are at the mercy of the stock market or property market fluctuations.

However, becoming a successful Online Entrepreneur is a path that not only leads to financial freedom so much more quickly (as explained most succinctly in the second half of MJ DeMarco's "Millionaire Fastlane: Crack The Code To Wealth & Live Rich For A Lifetime" but gives you back the control over your life from a very early stage in the game.

You will learn skills that nobody can ever take away from you and that gives you a strong feeling of power over your own destiny.

The low cost of starting a business, online, means that even if you were dumped in a new city without even a laptop, you could go to a public library (or borrow someone's smartphone) and start an online business again from scratch, becoming successful much more quickly probably, too!

James Schramko, an aussie entrepreneur who runs a multi-million dollar mentoring membership site recently got robbed while surfing on his last day in the USA – he literally had nothing but his board, a pair of flip-flops and his passport.

He was able to make his way to the airport, where he reported the car stolen, got online and onto Facebook and managed to get help, accommodation, clothes and then safely back to Australia within several days.

His stress levels, while high for a few hours, rapidly calmed down, he's lost a few things he didn't bother to replace, but his business carried on regardless, calmly making him money while he sorted things out
There is A Science To Getting Rich (& Doing That Online)

THERE is a science of getting rich, and it is an exact science, like algebra or arithmetic.

There is a science to making money online, and it is an exact science, like building a simple wall, adding one good brick on top of another.

Back to the riches part for a moment (I'll share the science of making money online in a while).

There are certain laws that govern the process of acquiring riches; once these laws are learned and obeyed by a person, they will get rich with mathematical certainty.

The creation of wealth and subsequent ownership of property and other "income producing assets" comes as a result of doing things in a certain way.

While each wealth generating route has some variations, there are generally accepted (within that particular industry) routes that work best, or fastest, or easiest.

Just as a baker, tailor, shoemaker, hotelier knows there are certain ways to run those businesses, a property investor, stock trader or internet marketer knows that there are a small number of certain ways to, if not ensure success, to maximise the chances of it.

Let's call this the "Certain Way" for now. You have to learn, understand and apply the rules, in order to succeed.

Once you have learned, understood and applied them you can start to think outside the box and try new things, but it's best done after you have used the short cuts others have created, rather than before.

Those who do things in their Certain Way, whether on purpose or accidentally, get rich; while those who do not do things in their Certain Way, no matter how hard they work or how able they are, remain poor.

It is a natural law that "like causes" always produce "like effects"; and, therefore, any person who learns to do things in that Certain Way will infallibly get rich.

That the above statement is true is shown by the following facts:

Getting rich is not a matter of environment, for, if it were, all the people in certain neighbourhoods would become wealthy; the people of one city would all be rich, while those of other towns would all be poor; or the inhabitants of one state would roll in wealth, while those of an adjoining state would be in poverty.

But, everywhere we see rich and poor living side by side, in the same environment, and often engaged in the same vocations.

When two men are in the same locality, and in the same business, and one gets rich while the other remains poor, it shows that getting rich is not, primarily, a matter of environment.

Some environments may be more favourable than others, but when two people in the same business are in the same neighbourhood, and one gets rich while the other fails, it indicates that getting rich is the result of doing things in a Certain Way.

And further, the ability to do things in their certain way is not due solely to the possession of talent, for some people who have great talent remain poor, while other who have very little talent get rich.

Studying the people who have got rich, we find that they are an average lot in all respects, having no greater talents and abilities than other men.

It is evident that they do not get rich because they possess talents and abilities that other men have not, but because they happen to do things in a Certain Way.

There's a great book called "Outliers" by Malcom Gladwell, that puts forward the "10,000 hours theory" that could explain why less talented people become more successful than the folks with the most immediately obvious talent.

Getting rich is not the result of saving, or "thrift" although many books like "The Millionaire Next Door" would have you think so.

Many very penny-pinching people are very poor, while free spenders often get rich.

People who won't invest in their own training and personal development for example, will rarely become rich while those who set aside a budget to travel to conferences where they will not only learn new skills and meet new people, will often become much wealthier over time, because of those activities.

Nor is getting rich due to doing things which others fail to do; for two men in the same business often do almost exactly the same things, and one gets rich while the other remains poor or becomes bankrupt.

From all these things, we must come to the conclusion that getting rich is the result of doing things in a Certain Way and that this Certain Way is more than just doing things in a certain way.

If getting rich is the result of doing certain things in a Certain Way, and if like causes always produce like effects, then any person who can do things in that way can become rich, and the whole matter is brought within the domain of exact science.

The question arises here, whether their Certain Way is so difficult that only a few may follow it. This cannot be true, as we have seen, so far as natural ability is concerned. Talented people get rich, and blockheads get rich; intellectually brilliant people get rich, and very stupid people get rich; physically strong people get rich, and weak and sickly people get rich.

Some degree of ability to think and understand is, of course, essential; but in so far natural ability is concerned, any person who has sense enough to read and understand these words can certainly get rich.

Also, we have seen that it is not a matter of environment. Location counts for something; one would not go to the heart of the Sahara and expect to do successful business.

Getting rich involves the necessity of dealing with people, and of being where there are enough people to deal with; and if these people are inclined to do business and buy in the way you want to sell, so much the better. But that is about as far as environment goes.

If anybody else in your town can get rich, so can you; and if anybody else in your state can get rich, so can you.

If anyone else who is 5' 10' with brown hair and blue eyes and a mole on their right forearm can get rich, then so can you.

The same goes for a 5' 4 blonde with green eyes and a slight deafness in your left ear…. well, you get the picture.

Again, it is not a matter of choosing some particular business or profession. People get rich in every business, and in every profession; while their next door neighbours in the same kind of business remain in poverty.

It is true that you will do best in a business which you like and find interesting, particularly if you are going to start a business online, and which is fun for you; and if you have certain talents which are well developed, you will do best in a business which calls for the use of those talents.

Here's a great diagram I used for months as my computer screensaver, while I was trying to decide what to do next, after The Money Gym closed.

Also, you will do best in a business which is suited to your location; an ice-cream parlor would do better in a warm climate than in Iceland, and a salmon fishery will succeed better in the Northwest than in Florida, where there are no salmon.

But, aside from these general limitations, getting rich is not dependent upon your engaging in some particular business, but upon your learning to do things in a Certain Way.

If you are now in business, and anybody else in your locality is getting rich in the same business, while you are not getting rich, it is because you are not doing things in the same Way that the other person is doing them.

No one is prevented from getting rich by lack of capital. Capital is spare cash that you have available to invest in a (hopefully) income producing asset.

So many people talk about having to raise capital or money to start a business.

What they actually mean is, they want someone to lend or give them the money to start a business so that that capital can pay them a salary!

True, as you get capital the increase becomes more easy and rapid; but one who has capital is already rich, and does not need to consider how to become so.

No matter how poor you may be, if you begin to do things in the Certain Way you will begin to get rich; and you will begin to have capital.

The acquiring of capital is a part of the process of getting rich; and it is a part of the result which invariably follows the doing of things in the Certain Way.

You may be the poorest person on the continent, and be deeply in debt; you may have neither friends, influence, nor resources; but if you begin to do things in the right way, you must infallibly begin to get rich, for like causes must produce like effects.

If you have no capital, you can get capital; if you are in the wrong business, you can get into the right business; if you are in the wrong location, you can go to the right location; and you can do so by beginning in your present business and in your present location to do things in the Certain Way which causes success.

Chapter 1: Recommended Resources:
Watch this amazing video featuring top psychologist Marisa Peer which will help you a lot if you are feeling that you don't deserve to be rich. Marisa is the most downloaded Mindvalley video ever so she must be striking a chord! We now have lipstick all over our mirrors, photo frames and even our fridge!

Is Opportunity Monopolised?

NO person is kept poor because opportunity has been taken away from him; because other people have monopolised the wealth, and have put a fence around it. You may be shut off from engaging in business in certain lines, but there are other channels open to you.

There are many industries that would appear to be pretty well monopolised, online, such as hosting and website building software.

But the gaming and app business for example is still in its infancy, and offers plenty of scope for enterprise; and offline, it will be many years until electric transportation, or wind power or clean water for all or the eradication of diseases like malaria by using simple practical tools are commonplace, and these industries will give employment to hundreds of thousands, if not millions, of people.

It is quite true that if you are employed by a big corporate you have very little chance of becoming the owner of the company in which you work; but it is also true that if you will commence to act in a Certain Way, you can soon leave the employment of that corporate; you can go and work for a brand new startup where you will be given equity (shares) in the company in return for working for a slightly lower salary for example.

There is great opportunity at this time for people who can learn to trade the stock markets, because you can make money while the markets are going up or going down, as long as you learn to read the signs and there are many good training courses that will teach you, online.

There is also a massive amount of opportunity to invest in real estate – even "no money down" like I did with my hotel - by creating problem solving deals for both the owners of the property, and folks who can't get a mortgage to buy.

This is called "Rent To Own" and it is happening in the USA, Canada, Australia and even more frequently in the UK. We are always a bit behind the USA!

You may say that it is impossible for you to invest in property, but I am going to prove to you that it is not impossible, and that you can certainly do it if you will go to work in a Certain Way.

That's how I bought a half million pound, 12 bedroom hotel "no money down" in 2003. Ironically, the same day I got the letter from the bank saying they were willing to lend me £250,000 (with no deposit) I got a letter from Virgin Credit Cards saying I hadn't been approved for a card for £1000.

The money game is played with different rules at different levels.

At different periods in man's history, the tide of opportunity sets in different directions, according to the needs of the whole, and the particular stage of social evolution, which has been reached.

At present, globally, the tide is firmly flowing towards information and technology and related industries and professions.

Opportunity is open to everyone regardless of background, schooling and influential contacts.

There is abundance of opportunity for the person who will go with the tide, and take advantage of it, instead of trying to swim against it.

So minimum wage workers, either as individuals or as a class, are not deprived of opportunity. The workers are not being "kept down" by their masters; they are not being "ground" by the corporates and wealthy.

As a group of people, they are where they are because they do not do things in a Certain Way. The minimum wage workers – those who work in pubs or restaurants, who work in shops or clean offices, who look after old people or children, may become successful entrepreneurs or property investors or stock market traders outside of their day jobs. Whenever they will begin to do things in a Certain Way; the law of wealth is the same for them as it is for all others.

This they must learn; but they will remain where they are as long as they continue to do as they do. The individual worker, however, is not held down by the ignorance or laziness of those around them; he can follow the tide of opportunity to riches, and this book will tell him how.

No one is kept in poverty by a shortness in the supply of riches; there is more than enough for all.

Remember that everything in life is made up of just a small number of just 90 elements and that there are inexhaustible supplies of those elements all around us.

Everything you see on earth – all the infinite variety of plant life and animals - is made from just a few original substances, the Building Blocks of Life which physics proves came from the stars, out of which all things are made, infused with the Life Force.

There is no limit to the supply of the Building Blocks Of Life. The universe is made out of it; but it was not all used up in making the universe.

The spaces in, through, and between the forms of the visible universe are permeated and filled with the Building Blocks Of Life; with the raw material of all things on the planet and in between those Building Blocks of Life is the thing that – although we don't yet know how or understand it fully - makes everything happen, the Life Force.

Many thousands, or even millions of times as much as has already been made, might still be made, and even then we should not have exhausted the supply of universal raw material.

No person, therefore, is poor because nature is poor, or because there is not enough to go around.

Nature is an inexhaustible storehouse of riches; yes, we must conserve some elements of it carefully, rainforests and woodlands and endangered species particularly, but the actual supply of the basic Building Blocks of Life will never run short.

The Building Blocks of Life along with the Life Force are also alive with creative energy, and are, with the help now of ever more creative people, constantly producing more things, new species, new variations of just about everything.

Things that did not exist even 100 years ago exist now.

For example, as we speak, in 2016, there are a million people travelling in the sky at any one time. There is a whole city up there in the sky right now and there is all the time.

Blows your mind a bit doesn't it?

Things that did not exist 50 years ago, like mobile phones and the internet, exist now. Things that did not exist 3 years ago, like electric cars that drive themselves and contact-less credit cards, exist now.

The Building Blocks Of Life respond to the needs of people; and the Life Force of those people. The Universe will not let us be without any good thing that we can imagine and then create by acting in a Certain Way.

This is true of people collectively; the race as a whole is always abundantly rich, and if individuals are poor, it is because they do not follow the Certain Way of doing things, the Way which makes the individual person rich.

For all we know, the Building Blocks Of Life and the Life Force is intelligent; it could be stuff which thinks.

We know so little yet of how the human mind works, what creates and fuels the thing we call the soul.

"We have no idea how widespread "intelligence" is in the cosmos. From our present knowledge, the most complex things in the Universe are ourselves, in particular, our brains. What's remarkable is that atoms have assembled into entities which are somehow able to ponder their origins" Sir Martin Rees, British cosmologist and astrophysicist, from the video "What We Still Don't Know: Are We Real?"

The same video goes on to wonder if we are real, or living in a massive simulation, created by someone, or something like a massive computer in a universe far, far away. But did that computer create itself and is it in a simulation too? Well worth watching that video all the way through and it helps if you have watched the Matrix films!

Part 2 of the video series asserts "Everything you thought you knew about the universe is wrong. It's made of atoms, right? Wrong. Atoms only account for a measly 15% of everything that exists. The mass of the universe consists of something so mysterious and elusive that it has been dubbed 'dark matter'".

Writing this in 2016, I have to wonder how Wallace D. Wattles could have possibly known that?

Let's get back to the subject in hand – can we impose our thoughts upon that "dark matter" or the Building Blocks of Life and Life Force, as I prefer to call it.

The numbers involved in the amount of calculations the brain makes every single second of every single day are just astonishing, I won't detail them here (there's a good list in my friend Andy Shaw's books "Creating A Bug Free Mind" and "Using A Bug Free Mind") but suffice to say, if we can do that in our little brains, what could be going on out there in the Universe, what gazillions of electrical impulses could be firing on all cylinders in the spaces between all of the Building Blocks Of Life?

We just can't stop seeking for more and trying to grow. It is the natural and inherent impulse of life to seek to live more; it is the nature of intelligence to enlarge itself, and of human consciousness to seek to extend its boundaries and find fuller expression.

The universe is inarguably a great Living Presence, on some level undetectable by us, yet always expanding and moving inherently toward more and bigger life.

You are not kept poor by lack in the supply of riches; you are kept poor by your unwillingness to expand, to seek more, to look to expand your knowledge and skills, by your refusal to believe, to come to know deep in your core, that you deserve more that you are achieving now.

The First Principle

We would like to put forward the theory – which seems to be born out by experience and nature, that your thoughts are in fact, the only power which can produce tangible riches from the Building Blocks Of Life and your own Life Force.

Consider this: Before someone thinks of something new, that thing does not exist.

Before I had the thought – just a couple of weeks ago, sitting in bed in Shoreham drinking my first coffee of the day actually - to rewrite this book "The Science Of Getting Rich" for the 21st Century, for people who want to create a business online, to include all the people who don't believe in a bearded deity sitting up in the sky, this book didn't exist anywhere in the universe.

Don't you find that thought really exciting? I do.

The energy from which all things are made – their Life Force – begins in the place where people think, and a thought of a thing with enough life force behind it, almost inevitably produces the thing.

There is a word called "Zeitgeist" which means spirit of the times. This word explains why three sets of people were working on the theory and practicality of flight at the same time. It also goes some way to explain why all the fashion designers – secretive about their new collections to a person - suddenly decide that the 1980's are once again cool and this year all the fashionistas should wear 80's fashion again!

From the Wikipedia entry for zeitgeist: "Executives, venture capitalists, journalists and authors have argued that the idea of a zeitgeist is useful in understanding the emergence of industries, simultaneous invention and evaluating the relative value of innovations. Malcolm Gladwell argued in his book Outliers that entrepreneurs who succeeded often share similar characteristics—early personal or significant exposure to knowledge and skills in the early stages of a nascent industry. He proposed that the timing of involvement in an industry and often in sports as well affected the probability of success. In Silicon Valley, a number of people (Peter Thiel, Alistair Davidson, Mac Levchin, Nicholas G. Carr, Vinod Khosla) have argued that much of the current (2014) innovation has been shaped by easy access to the Internet, open source software, component technologies for both hardware and software (e.g., software libraries, SaaS), and the ability to reach narrow markets across a global market"

In other words, people who come up with great ideas at the same time, even when they don't know each other at all, are experiencing the same input of data and then their brains take that data and leapt to similar conclusions and then they make the thing that they are thinking about, real.

My thought of this book, created in my brain which is made up of the Building Blocks Of Life, which is driven by my Life Force, produced the thing. This book now exists.

The chair I'm sitting on, the computer I'm using to type these words, the granola I had for breakfast, the bowl I ate it out of....all of those things did not exist once, but now they do, as a direct result of someone having an idea and then somehow, making that idea take shape in physical form.

We can take a leap and imagine that every form and process you see in nature is the visible expression of some kind of thought (even if we don't yet know how that thought works) in the Building Blocks of Life and the Life Force of the Universe.

As the Building Blocks Of Life and the Life Force "thinks" of a form, it takes that form; as it thinks of a motion, it makes that motion. Thinking of a tree makes a tree, thinking of an ocean, makes an ocean.

That is the way all of the useful objects in our world were created so is it too far of a stretch to think that some form of intelligence is working out there to create everything else we see. You could say we live in a thought driven world, which is part of a thought driven universe.

Somehow, the Building Blocks Of Life and the Life Force created a moving universe, whole systems of planets, every thing on those planets and somehow it all maintains those forms that we see around us (and some that which we can't see yet).

Perhaps, by holding the idea of a circling system of suns and worlds, the Building Blocks Of Life and Life Force takes the form of these bodies, and moves them as it thinks. Thinking the form of a slow-growing oak tree, the Life Force moves accordingly, and produces the tree, though centuries may be required to do the work.

In creating once, the Life Force then seems to move according to the lines of motion it has established before; the thought of an oak tree does not cause the instant formation of a full- grown tree, but it does start in motion the forces which will produce the tree, along established lines of growth.

Over and over again.

Every thought of form, held in thinking Substance, causes the creation of the form, generally, along lines of growth and action already established.

The idea or thought of a house of a certain construction, if it were just an idea in someone's head, an architect or keen home builder for example, might not cause the instant formation, of the house; but it would cause the turning of creative energies already working in the building industry into such channels as to result in the speedy building of the house.

And if there were no existing channels through which the creative energy could work, then the idea of the house would be formed and someday, when conditions are right, it would be created in the world that we can see, touch and feel.

Just look back to the pictures of the modern home, imagined by the people in the middle of the last century. All your security, heating, blinds, hot water and entertainment systems controlled from one portable gadget? The houses and apps are here, in some people's lives and smart phones already.

People are thinking centres, and can originate thought. All the things that people make with their hands must first exist in their thought; you cannot shape a thing until you have thought of that thing.

And so far you have probably confined your efforts to succeed wholly to the kind of work most people around you do; you may have had a few thoughts about how to do those jobs better, or possibly even about how to take an existing business model and copy that, or adapt it in some way.

You haven't thought of trying to create new things or business models by turning your thoughts to the use of the Building Blocks Of Life and your own Life Force.

You have, so far, made little or no effort to work with – to create success using - the Building Blocks of Life or your own Life Force.

You have given no attention to the question of whether you may not produce things from The Building Blocks Of Life and your Life Force by simply communicating your thoughts and desires to it.

I will endeavour to prove that you may do so; to prove that any person may do so, and to show you how.

As our first step, we must lay down three basic ideas.

First, that there is such a thing as the "dark matter" or the Building Blocks Of Life, from which all things are made.

All the seemingly many elements are but different presentations of one element; all the many forms found in organic and inorganic nature are but different shapes, made from the same stuff, drawn from the 90 different chemical compounds known to the scientists.

And that something within that stuff might be capable of doing something that could be described as holding a thought, which produces the shape of the thing that is made of that stuff.

Simply put, that the Thought, within the Building Blocks of Life, produces things.

If a person is a thinking centre, capable of original thought; then if a person can somehow communicate their thought to The Building Blocks of Life and their Life Force, then you can cause the creation, or formation, of the thing, the desire, you are thinking about.

To summarise that -- There are Building Blocks Of Life infused with a Life Force, from which all things are made, and which, in its original state, permeates, penetrates, and fills the interspaces of the Universe.

A type of thought, in those Building Blocks Of Life infused with a Life Force, produces the thing that is imaged by the thought.

People can create things in their own thought, and, by somehow communicating your thought to the Building Blocks of Life and the Life Force, can cause the thing you think about to be created.

It may be asked if I can prove these statements; and without going into details right now, I answer that I can do so, both by logic and experience.

Thinking about the sciences of chemistry, physics and biology, and how we are all formed – how everything is formed – from the same few elements of the 90 at the disposal of the Universal Energy, the Building Blocks Of Life infused with the very obvious Life Force, thinking about the phenomena of form and thought and creation, I come to believe, no, I come to know a person's power to create the formation of the thing he thinks about.

Good things and bad things.

And from my own life experience, and by watching the life experiences of the many successful AND unsuccessful people around me, I find the reasoning true; and that is my strongest proof.

If one person who reads this book gets rich by doing what it tells them to do, that is evidence in support of my claim; but if every person who reads it and then does what it tells them to do, gets rich, that is positive proof until some one goes through the process and fails.

The theory is true until the process fails; and the process will not fail, for every person who does exactly what this book tells them to do, will get rich.

I have said that we can get rich by doing things in a Certain Way; and in order to be able to do things in the Certain Way, we must become able to think in a certain way.

Therefore, a person's way of doing things is the direct result of the way they think about things.

To do things in a way you want to do them, you will have to acquire the ability to think in the way you want to think; this is the first step toward getting rich.

You must get control of your own mind. Not just once, but all the time. The good news is, that it gets easier and easier with practice.

To think what you want to think, is to think the TRUTH, based on what you have learned so far in this book, regardless of external appearances.

Every person has the natural and inherent power to think what he wants to think, but it requires far more effort to do so than it does to simply think the thoughts which are suggested by appearances.

Example: If you have no money in your bank account at the moment you may think you are poor but you are not poor. You are rich in many things but you may be just broke temporarily.

To think according to appearance is easy; to think truth regardless of appearances is hard work, and requires the expenditure of more mind power than any other "normal" person is usually called upon to perform.

There is no work from which most people avoid as much as they do from that of using sustained and logical thought; it is the hardest work in the world.

This is especially true when the Truth is contrary to appearances.

Every appearance in the visible world tends to produce a corresponding form in your mind which observes it; and this can only be prevented by constantly holding the thought of the TRUTH.

To look upon the appearances of poverty will produce corresponding forms in your own mind, unless you hold to the Truth that there is no poverty; there is only abundance.

To think health when surrounded by the appearances of disease, or to think riches when in the midst of appearances of poverty, requires substantial practice in developing your mind power; but you, when you acquire this power, you will become a MASTER MIND.

You can conquer fate; you can have what you want.

This power can only be acquired by embracing the basic fact which is behind all appearances; and that fact is that there is one Substance, from which all of the Building Blocks Of Life and by use of those, which all things are made.

Then we must grasp the truth that every thought held long enough and powerfully enough becomes a form, and that you can so impress your thoughts upon it as to cause them to take form and become visible things.

When we realise this, we lose all doubt and fear, for we know that we can create what we want to create; we can get what we want to have, and can become what we want to be.

As a first step toward getting rich, you must believe the three fundamental statements given previously in this chapter; and in order to emphasise them.

I repeat them here:--

There are a small number of Building Blocks Of Life infused with Life Force, which is intelligent in it's own right, from which all things are made, and which permeates, penetrates, and fills the interspaces of the universe.

A thought, created in my mind but powerfully communicated to those Building Blocks of Life and infused with my Life Force, will inevitably produce the thing that I desire and which is represented by that thought.

People can form things in their thoughts and by thinking powerfully and positively about those things as if they have already happened, can cause the thing they are thinking about to be created.

If this sounds right and true to you, you must go further than just believing it, you must KNOW it to be true and live every second of your life, like you know it.

You must forget all other concepts of the Universe than this one; and you must think about this one until it is indelibly fixed in your mind, and has become your only thought.

Read these "end of chapter" statements over and over again; fix every word upon your memory, and meditate upon them until you firmly believe what they say.

If a doubt comes to you, and they will, they will, cast it aside and remember that, in the words of Mike Dooley from TUT "Thoughts become things, think good ones!".

Do not read magazines or books which teach a different idea; if you get mixed up in your thoughts, all your efforts will be in vain. Do not ask why these things are true, nor speculate as to how they can be true; if they feel right, simply take them on trust.

People have been doing that for nearly 100 years now, since this book was first published and it's worked for them without any of the scientific backup that's becoming available now.

Just do a search on YouTube using the phrase "The Secret" and you will find people like Will Smith, Oprah, Kanye West, Pharrell Williams, Jay-Z and many, many more mega successful people believe in this principle and apply it to their lives.

The science of getting rich for you begins with the absolute acceptance of the contents of this book, which is being increasingly backed up by the very top scientist's studies of chemistry, biology and physics.

Increasing Life & Creating Abundance)

Now. I don't know how you were brought up, but I was lucky enough to have been brought up in a house where religion was barely mentioned, although we were brought up with strong personal values.

Even if you were not, and you currently believe in a Deity and want to continue doing so, you must get rid of the last vestiges of the old idea that there is a Deity whose will it is that you should be poor, or that you are a better, more pious person if you are poor, or that it's purposes may be better served by keeping you in poverty.

Every living thing must continually seek for the enlargement of its life, because life, in the mere act of living, must increase itself.

Put simply, if you are not growing you are dying. As Woody Allen famously put it, if you are a shark or a relationship, if you are not moving forward, you'll die.

A seed, dropped into the ground, springs into activity, and in the act of living produces a hundred more seeds; life, by living, multiplies itself. It is forever Becoming More; it must do so, if it continues to be at all.

Thinking about lack and scarcity produces more lack and scarcity, thinking about increasing of life and abundance creates more abundance.

Intelligence is under the same necessity for continuous increase. Every thought we think makes it necessary for us to think another thought; consciousness is continually expanding.

Every fact we learn leads us to the learning of another fact; knowledge is continually increasing. Every talent we cultivate brings to the mind the desire to cultivate another talent; we are subject to the urge of life, seeking expression, which ever drives us on to know more, to do more, and to be more.

This might sound overwhelming initially, but the best thing about creating a business online, is that you learn and then use one skill to create one part of the whole, then you can learn another skill which creates another part of the whole, over and over again, until the whole business sits on the internet, working for you, increasing your overall wealth.

You will know more, do things once and then you'll be more and have more. You don't have to keep doing more, over and over again!

In order to know more, do more, and be more we must have more; we must have things to use, for we learn, and do, and become, only by using things. We must get rich, so that we can live more fully.

The desire for riches is simply the capacity for larger life seeking fulfilment; every desire is the effort of an, as yet, unexpressed possibility to come into action.

It is the Life Force seeking to manifest itself in you which causes desire. That desire, which makes you want more money is the same as that which makes the plant grow; it is Life, seeking fuller expression.

The Building Blocks of Life infused with the Life Force between must be subject to the inherent law of all life; it is permeated with the desire to live more; that is why it is under the necessity of creating things.

The Building Blocks of Life and the Life Force that's in all of us, desires to live even more fully in you; hence it wants you to have all the things you can use to live more fully yourself.

It is the desire of every thing that makes up Universal Energy that you expand your potential, that you should get rich.

We can extrapolate from the previous thoughts in this book that The Universe desires you to have everything you want to have. Nature is friendly to your plans.

Everything is there naturally for you. Make up your mind that this is true.

It is essential, however that your purpose in wanting more, should harmonise with the purpose that is in everything.

Life is the performance of function; and someone only really lives when they perform every function, physical, mental, and spiritual, of which they are capable, without over excess in any.

Balance is key.

You do not want to get rich in order to enjoy purely physical pleasures; that is not life. But the performance of every physical function is a part of life, and no one lives completely who denies the impulses of the body a normal and healthful expression.

You do not want to get rich solely to enjoy mental pleasures, to get knowledge, to gratify ambition, to outshine others, to be famous. All these are a legitimate part of life, but the person who lives for the pleasures of the intellect alone will only have a partial life, and they will never be satisfied with their portion.

You do not want to get rich solely for the good of others, to lose yourself for the salvation of humankind, to experience only the joys of philanthropy and sacrifice. The joys of the soul are only a part of life; and they are no better or nobler than any other part.

You want to get rich in order that you may eat, drink, and be merry when it is time to do these things and have the control and respect for yourself to abstain when it is not; in order that you may surround yourself with beautiful things, see distant lands, feed your mind, and develop your intellect; in order that you may love other people and do kind things, and be able to play a good part in helping the world to find their truth.

But remember that extreme altruism is no better and no nobler than extreme selfishness; both are distractions and mistakes.

Get rid of the idea that Universal Energy wants you to sacrifice yourself for others, and that you can secure anyone's favour by doing so; Universal Energy requires nothing of the kind.

What Universal Energy "wants", it would appear, is that you should make the most of yourself, for yourself, and for others; and you can help others more by making the most of yourself than in any other way.

You can make the most of yourself only by getting rich; so as to be able to easily afford the things that will help you do that, so it is perfectly fine that you should give your first and best thought to the work of acquiring wealth.

Remember, however, that this focus and movement towards your wealth must be for more life to all; it cannot be made to work for less life to any, because it is equally in all, seeking riches and life.

The Building Blocks of Life and Life Force, communicated to well and used right, will make things for you, but will not take things away from some one else and give them to you.

You must get rid of the thought of competition. You are to create abundance, not to compete for what is already created by other people.

You do not have to take anything away from any one. You do not have to drive hard bargains. You do not have to cheat, or to take advantage. You do not need to let any person work for you for less than he earns for you.

You do not have to covet the property of others, or to look at it with wishful eyes; no person has anything of which you cannot have the same, and by having that without taking what you have away from him.

You are to become a creator, not a competitor; you are going to get what you want, but in such a way that when you get it every other person will have more than you have now.

I am aware that there are people who get a vast amount of money by proceeding in direct opposition to the statements in the paragraph above, and may add a word of explanation here.

Some people, arrogant people, who become very rich, do so sometimes purely by their extraordinary ability in imposing their will on others, or competing with others and taking by competition.

The great entrepreneurs of the last couple of centuries, Rockefeller, Carnegie, Gates, Jobs et al., have been the unconscious agents of the Life Force in the necessary work of systematising and organising industry and information; and while some of the earlier entrepreneurs in particular may have used the force of competition, in the end, their work will contribute immensely toward an increased quality of life for all.

As we move into the 21st Century now, the more generally accepted way of successfully doing things is by collaboration, not competition.

The multi -millionaires of the late 18th and early 19th Century who did act like that are like the monster reptiles of the prehistoric eras; they play a necessary part in the evolutionary process, but the same competitive power which produced them will dispose of them.

And it is well to bear in mind that they have never been really rich; a record of the private lives of most of their kind will show that they have really been the most and wretched of the poor, emotionally speaking.

Riches secured on using competitive power are never satisfactory and permanent; they are yours today, and another person's tomorrow.

Remember, if you are to become rich in a scientific and certain way, you must rise entirely out of the competitive thought process.

You must never think for a moment that the supply is limited.

Just as soon as you begin to think that all the money is being "cornered" and controlled by corrupt governments, bankers and others, and that you must exert yourself to get laws passed to stop their process, and so on; in that moment you drop into the competitive mind, and your power to cause creation is gone for the time being; and what is worse, you will probably stop all the creative movements towards wealth you have already started.

Physical money is just a thing that represents energy. The energy of one person doing something for another. We don't even use real money much any more, in our day to day lives which makes it easier to think of it as just a unit of energy.

Know that money is just an way of keeping track of exchanges of energy. There are billions and billions of dollars (the international symbol for exchanges of energy) sloshing around the world electronically right now. An ocean of virtual money.

That ocean is getting ever bigger as banks literally "make" more money, however they are not creating wealth because they are not creating anything, just printing more units of keeping track of future exchanges of energy.

By building your own online business, by solving the problems or enabling the passions of the millions and millions of people right now, you will be able to dip a teaspoon initially into that ocean and, by providing exceptional value to someone out there in the world right now, looking for what you will provide, you'll be able to turn that teaspoon into a bucket into a hosepipe!

Never, ever look at the visible supply of money; what is in your bank account right now, and think "that's it!".

Look always at the limitless riches sloshing around the world and that you can tap into by using your Building Blocks Of Life and your own Life Force, and KNOW that riches and the things that those riches can buy are coming to you as fast as you can receive and use them.

Nobody, by cornering the visible supply, can prevent you from getting what is yours now and is on it's way to you if you just do things in the Certain Way.

So never allow yourself to think for an instant that all the best building spots will be taken before you get ready to build your house, unless you hurry. Never worry about the corporates, and get anxious for fear they will soon come to own the whole earth.

Never get afraid that you will lose what you want because some other person "beats you to it." That cannot possibly happen; you are not seeking any thing that is possessed by anybody else; you are causing what you want to be created from the Building Blocks of Life, and the Life Force supply is without limits.

Remember....

There are a small number of Building Blocks Of Life infused with Life Force, which is intelligent in it's own right, from which all things are made, and which permeates, penetrates, and fills the interspaces of the universe.

A thought, created in my mind but powerfully communicated to those Building Blocks of Life and infused with my Life Force, will inevitably produce the thing that I desire and which is represented by that thought.

People can form things in their thoughts and by thinking powerfully and positively about those things as if they have already happened, can cause the thing they are thinking about to be created.

How Riches Come to You

WHEN I say that you do not have to drive hard bargains, I do not mean that you do not have to drive any bargains at all, or that you are above the necessity for having any dealings with your fellow men.

I don't mean you'll never have to make a sale!

I mean that you will not need to deal with them unfairly; you do not have to try and get something for nothing, but can give to every person more value than you take from him.

A good rule of thumb online is to try and give 10x more value than you are charging and it's easier to do it online because you simply don't have all the overheads that a physical business has.

You can host your videos for free online at YouTube, you can host PDF's and ebooks on your website or, if you are anticipating a lot of downloads, you can host things on Amazon S3 for pennies and only pay that, when people actually download them.

Most of the tools are available to use for a tiny amount per month, when compared with the expenses of running a "real world" business.

A full suite of those tools, using the very "best of breed" versions will not cost you more than around $500 a month while you can get started for pretty much the cost of your domain name and hosting - under $10 a month.

If you are selling physical products, for example on Amazon, you cannot give every person more in cash market value than you take from him, but you can give him more in use value than the cash value of the thing you take from him.

If you had bought this book in paperback or hardback version, the value of the paper, ink, and other material in this book may not be worth the money you pay for it; but if the ideas suggested by it bring you thousands of dollars, you have not been ripped off by those who sold it to you; they have given you a great use in value for a small cash value.

Let us suppose that I own a picture by one of the great artists, which, in any civilised community, is worth thousands of dollars. I take it to a great auction house or wholesaler, and by "salesmanship" induce you, an Eskimo to give me a bundle of furs worth $500 for it.

In that transaction, I have really wronged him, for while you have got a bargain (the picture is worth many thousands of dollars after all) you have no use for the picture; it has no use value to you; it will not add to your life.

But suppose I give you a gun worth $50 for your $500 worth of furs; then you have made a good bargain. You have great use for the gun; it will make your life easier, it will get you many more furs and much food; it will add to your life in every way; it will make you rich, in your terms.

When you rise from the competitive to the creative plane, you can look at your business transactions very strictly, and if you are selling any person anything which does not add more to their life than the thing he give you in exchange, you can afford to stop it.

You do not have to beat anybody in business. And if you are in a business which does beat or scam people, get out of it at once.

Remember, give every person more in use value than you take from him in cash value; then you are adding to the life of the world by every business transaction.

If you have people working for you, you must take from them more in cash value than you pay them in wages; but you can so organise your business that it will be filled with the principle of advancement, and so that each employee who wishes to do so, may improve his skills, knowledge and experience a little every day.

It's a good time now to mention Outsourcing. This means the practice of when you hire someone who has the skills and talent you need, but perhaps they live in a country where the cost of living is way below that of the country where you live.

Hiring software developers in Eastern Europe for example, or Virtual Assistants or Graphic Designers in the Philippines can be unbelievably inexpensive compared to what the people charge for the same skills at home.

Many people are highly resistant to this idea, feeling somehow that they are ripping these people off, or that they should be hiring in their own country.

Think about if for a second, though. If you could only hire more expensively in your own country for the job, and that meant your business would not succeed, so would not exist, how are you increasing life if you are not increasing your business and spreading that abundance around the world?

Surely, from what you are learning in this book, deep down inside you now, you know that inevitably the abundance you spread in the Philippines or Eastern Europe, will make it's way back to the USA or the UK, wherever you are based.

My own Virtual Assistant Chachie said to me recently, after I referred one of my own clients to her "Thank you so much, you don't know what a difference this work is making, not just to me and my family, but to my whole village!"

Don't' forget, you can make your business do for your employees what this book is doing for you.

You can conduct your business that it will be a sort of ladder, by which every employee who will take the trouble may climb to riches himself; and given the opportunity, if he will not do so it is not your fault.

And finally, because you are to cause the creation of your riches from The Building Blocks Of Life which permeates all your environment, it does not follow that they are to take shape from the atmosphere and come into being before your eyes.

If you want a sewing machine, for instance, I do not mean to tell you that you are to impress the thought of a sewing machine on The Building Blocks Of Life until the machine is formed without hands, in the room where you sit, or elsewhere.

But if you want a sewing machine, hold the mental image of it with the most positive certainty that it is being made somewhere, or is on its way to you.

After once forming the thought, have the most absolute and unquestioning faith that the sewing machine is coming; never think of it, or speak, of it, in any other way than as being sure to arrive. Claim it in your head and your heart as if it's already yours.

It will be brought to you by the power of the Universal Energy, acting upon the minds of men. If you live in Maine, it may be that a person will be brought from Texas or Japan to engage in some transaction with you which will result in your getting that sewing machine you want.

If so, the whole matter will be as much to that person's advantage as it is to yours.

I managed to manifest a car like this; just after I was made bankrupt, I knew I wanted a car that I would pay for in instalments, without a big deposit, and no credit checks. I started to put the feelers out for a car dealership that would perhaps lend or rent me a car in return for internet marketing services.

A couple of weeks later, my friend Susanne Jorgensen called me and said she was moving back to America for a year and did I want to rent her car?

When I went to pick it up, I was staggered to see that it was a silver Mercedes convertible, nearly identical to the one on my dream-board!

Here's me sitting in it with the top down in the sunshine on the first day, feeling a bit self-conscious but enjoying every minute.

My only unexpected challenge now was that it was only a two-seater, and I have two large teens to fit in. When I looked at my dream-board that car I had torn out of a magazine only had two seats too!

It really was very, very spooky and taught me that I should have been more specific!

So now I have a gorgeous Audi soft-top with 4 seats on my dream-board.

Do not forget for a moment that Universal Energy working through The Building Blocks Of Life infused with Life Force is through all, in all, communicating with all, and can influence all.

The desire of Universal Energy for fuller life and better living has caused the creation of all the sewing machines already made, all the silver convertible Mercedes ever made; and it can cause the creation of millions more, and will, whenever men set it in motion by desire and faith, and by acting in a Certain Way.

You can certainly have a Mercedes in your garage; and it is just as certain that you can have any other thing you want, and which you will use for the advancement of your own life and the lives of others.

You need not hesitate about asking big, Universal Energy wants to live all that is possible in you, and wants you to have all that you can, or will use for the living of the most abundant life possible.
If you fix upon your consciousness the fact that the desire you feel for the possession of riches is one with the desire of Universal Energy for more complete expression, your faith becomes invincible.

Once I saw a little boy sitting at a piano, and vainly trying to bring harmony out of the keys; and I saw that he was grieved and provoked by their inability to play real music. I asked him the cause of his frustration, and he answered, "I can feel the music in me, but I can't make my hands go right." The music in him was the URGE of Universal Energy, containing all the possibilities of all life; all that there is of music was seeking expression through the child.

Universal Energy, the One Substance, could be described as trying to live and do and enjoy things through humanity.

"I want hands to build wonderful structures, to play divine harmonies, to paint glorious pictures; I want feet to explore, eyes to see beauties, tongues to tell mighty truths and to sing marvellous songs".

All that there is of possibility is seeking expression through us.

Universal Energy wants those who can play music to have pianos and tuition and every other instrument, and to have the means to cultivate their talents to the fullest extent; it wants those who can appreciate beauty to be able to surround themselves with beautiful things; it wants those who can discern truth to have every opportunity to travel and observe; those who can appreciate dress to be beautifully clothed, and those who can appreciate good food and wine to be luxuriously dined.

Can you think of a time when you experienced doing any of those things, remember the soaring and majestic feelings you felt, the connection to Life itself you experienced in that moment.

That was your connection with the Universal Energy.

Similarly the desire you feel for riches is Universal Energy, seeking through the Building Blocks Of Life to connect the Life Force of the Universe to your own Life Force, seeking to express itself in you as He sought to find expression in the little boy at the piano.

So you need not hesitate to ask big and keep asking big.

Your part is to focus, get specific and express your desire to Universal Energy.

And we call them desires because it's a more powerful word than "want" or "need" and it doesn't imply an ongoing state of that thing.

If you want, you will always want, if you need, you will always need, but if your desire, that's a whole other thing indeed.

This asking big and keeping asking big is a difficult point with most people; they retain something of the old idea that poverty and self-sacrifice are pleasing to Universal Energy. They look upon poverty as a part of the plan, a necessity of nature.

They have the idea that Universal Energy has finished its' work, and made all that it can make, and that the majority must stay poor because there is not enough to go around. They hold to so much of this wrong and scarce thinking that they feel ashamed to ask for wealth; they try not to want more than a very modest amount, just enough to make them fairly comfortable.

I recall now the case of one student who was told that he must get in mind a clear picture of the things he desired, so that the creative thought of them might be impressed on Universal Energy.

He was a very poor person, living in a rented house, and having only what he earned from day to day; and he could not grasp the fact that all wealth was there for the taking.

So, after thinking the matter over, he decided that he might reasonably ask for a new rug for the floor of their best room, and a coal stove to heat the house during the cold weather.

Following the instructions given in this book, he obtained these things in a few months; and then it dawned upon him that he had not asked enough.

He went through the house in which he lived, and planned all the improvements he would like to make in it; he mentally added a bay window here and a room there, until it was complete in their mind as their ideal home; and then he planned its furnishings.

Holding the whole picture in their mind, he began living in the Certain Way, and moving toward what he wanted; and he owns the house now, and is rebuilding it after the form of their mental image.

And now, with still larger faith, he is going on to get greater things.

It has been given to him because of his faith that it will work, and it is so with you, and with all of us.

Gratitude

THE illustrations given in the last chapter will have conveyed to you the fact that the first step toward getting rich is to convey the idea of your desires to the Universal Energy.

This is true, and you will see that in order to do so, it becomes necessary to communicate your desires to Universal Energy in a pleasing, harmonious way so that you are aligned and can vibrate at the right frequency to achieve your goals.

To do it like this is a matter of such vital importance that I shall give you instructions which, if you will follow them, will be certain to bring you into perfect unity of mind with Universal Energy.

The whole process of mental adjustment and atonement and tuning yourself up the right vibrational frequency can be summed up in one word, gratitude.

First, you believe – no, you KNOW - that there is one Universal Energy, from which all things proceed; second, you know that this Universal Energy can give you everything you desire; and third, you relate yourself to Universal Energy by a feeling of deep and profound gratitude.

Many people who are doing everything else right in all other ways are kept in poverty by their lack of gratitude. Having received one gift from Universal Energy, they cut the wires which connect them with it by failing to make proper acknowledgment by giving thanks, by feeling deep gratitude.

It is easy to understand that the nearer we live to the source of wealth, the more wealth we shall receive; and it is easy also to understand that the soul that is always grateful lives in closer touch with Universal Energy than the one which never expresses thankful acknowledgment.

The more gratefully we fix our minds on the Universal Energy when good things come to us, the more good things we will receive, and the more rapidly they will come; and the reason simply is that the mental attitude of gratitude draws the mind into closer touch with the Universal Energy and Life Source from which the blessings come.

If it is a new thought to you that gratitude brings your whole mind into closer harmony with the creative energies of the universe, consider it deeply over the next few days, and you will see that it is true.

It is the secret of true happiness.

You try feeling sad or mad with anyone while you are thinking, and ideally writing out, all the things you are grateful for!

The good things you already have, have come to you along the line of obedience to certain laws. Gratitude will lead your mind out along the ways by which things come; and it will keep you in close harmony with creative thought and prevent you from falling into competitive thought. Gratitude alone can keep you looking toward Universal Energy and keep you feeling abundant, and prevent you from falling into the error of thinking of the supply of the Building Blocks Of Life as scarce or limited; because to do that would be fatal to your hopes.

There is a Law of Gratitude, and it is absolutely necessary that you should observe the law, if you are to get the results you seek.

The Law of Gratitude is the natural principle that action and reaction are always equal, and in opposite directions.

Gratitude is so attractive, it makes the most mighty and powerful seem pleasantly humble and draws people to them. Why do you think people love Oprah – one of the most powerful women in television - so much? She practices gratitude all the time and exudes an authentic attitude of humbleness.

One of my heroes is Gary Vaynerchuk and while he's a "Marmite" kind of guy and not everyone gets on with his cussing, you can't argue with the fact that he's always grateful, to his parents, to being brought up in America, to the fact his Mom gave his so much love and attention he didn't' feel a failure when he got straight F's at school, that the internet came along at the right time for him to make his mark.

The grateful outreaching of your mind in thankful praise to the Universal Energy is a powerful liberation of vibration or an expenditure of Life Force; it cannot fail to reach that to which it addressed, and the reaction is an instantaneous movement towards you.

And if your gratitude is strong and constant, the reaction in the Building Blocks of Life will be strong and continuous; the movement of the things you want will be always toward you, never away from you.

While I've been re-writing and editing this book, over the last week several miraculous things have happened in my business, because I'm steeped neck deep in these principles at the moment, living, sleeping, eating and breathing them, I must be giving off major vibrational power and attraction!

You cannot exercise or project much power without gratitude; for it is gratitude that keeps you connected with your Power (but not in slavery to the idea of it).

But the value of gratitude does not consist solely in getting you more blessings in the future. Without gratitude you cannot long keep from dissatisfied thought regarding things as they are.

The moment you permit your mind to dwell with dissatisfaction upon things as they are, you begin to lose ground.

You fix attention upon the common, the shabby, the ordinary, the poor, and the squalid and mean; and your mind takes the form of these things. Then you will transmit these forms or mental images to Universal Energy, and more of the the common, the poor, the shabby, the squalid, and mean will come to you.

To permit your mind to dwell upon the inferior around you, is to become inferior yourself and to surround yourself with inferior things.

On the other hand, to fix your attention on the best that surrounds you is to surround yourself mentally and emotionally with the best, and to become the best yourself.

The Creative Power within us makes us into the image of that to which we most give our attention.

We are the Building Blocks Of Life and Life Force, and the Building Blocks Of Life always takes the form of that which it most thinks about.
The grateful mind is constantly fixed upon the best; therefore it tends to become the best; it takes the form or character of the best, and will receive the best.

Also, knowing that this works is born of gratitude. The grateful mind continually expects good things, and expectation becomes knowing. The reaction of gratitude upon one's own mind produces more knowing; and every outgoing wave of grateful thanksgiving increases that knowing.

If you have no feeling of gratitude you cannot for long retain a living feeling of knowing; and without a living feeling of knowing that it all works, you cannot get rich by the creative method, as we shall see in the following chapters.

It is necessary, then, to cultivate the habit of being grateful for every good thing that comes to you; and to give thanks continuously.

And because all the things that have happened to you so far and that surround you now, have contributed to your potential, and to your reading this book, you should include all of those things in your gratitude.

Do not waste time thinking or talking about the shortcomings or wrong actions of others. Their place in the world has made your opportunity; all you get, really comes to you because of them too.

Do not rage against corrupt politicians; if it were not for politicians we should fall into anarchy, and your opportunity for becoming more would be greatly lessened.

Universal Energy has worked a long time and very patiently to bring us up to where we are in industry and government, and is continuing to do so.

There is not the least doubt that one day, when we are ready, when enough people are taking responsibility for themselves, their lives and their families, we will do away with plutocrats, trust magnates, captains of industry, and politicians as soon as they can be spared; but in the meantime, try and be grateful that most of them are doing the best they can.

Remember that they are all helping to arrange the lines of manufacture and transportation along which your riches will come to you, and be grateful to them all rather than writing more posts on Facebook about how corrupt it all is.

This will bring you into harmonious relations with the good in everything, and the good in everything will move toward you.

Thinking in the Certain Way

TURN back to chapter 6 and read again the story of my car that I manifested, so perfect in every way except one, also the person who formed a mental image of their house, and you will get a fair idea of the initial steps toward getting rich.

You must form a clear and definite mental picture of what you want; you cannot transmit an idea unless you have it clear in your mind yourself.

You must have it clear in your mind before you can give it; and many people fail to impress their desires upon Universal Energy, the Building Blocks of Life and the Life Force because they have themselves only a vague and misty concept of the things they want to do, to have, or to become.

It is not enough that you should have a general desire for wealth "to do good with"; everybody has that desire.

It is not enough that you should have a wish to travel, see things, live more, etc. Everybody has those desires also.

If you were going to send an email to a friend, you would not send the letters of the alphabet in their right order, and let him construct the message for himself; nor would you take words at random from the dictionary.

You would send a series of coherent sentence; one which meant something.

When you try to impress your wants upon Universal Energy, the Building Blocks of Life and the Life Force, remember that it must be done by a coherent statement; you must know what you want, and be definite.

You can never get rich, or start the creative power into action, by sending out unformed longings and vague desires.

Go over your desires just as I did with my dream-board, just as the person I have described went over their house; see just what you want, and get a clear mental picture of it as you wish it to look when you get it.

Then go back and look again, making sure that ALL the details are exactly as you desire them!

That clear mental picture you must have continually in mind, as the sailor has in mind the port toward which he is sailing the ship; you must keep your face toward it all the time. You must no more lose sight of it than the Captain loses sight of the compass.

It is not necessary to take exercises in concentration, nor to set apart special times for affirmation, nor to "go into the silence," nor to do weird stunts of any kind.

All you need is to know what you desire, and to desire it badly enough so that it will stay in your thoughts.

Spend as much of your leisure time as you can in writing out your desires or contemplating your pictures, but no one needs to take exercises to concentrate their mind on a thing which he really wants; it is the things you do not really care that much about which require a huge effort to fix your attention upon them.

And unless you really want to get rich, so that the desire is strong enough to hold your thoughts directed to the purpose as the magnetic pole holds the needle of the compass, it will hardly be worth while for you to try to carry out the instructions given in this book.

The methods in this book are for people whose desire for riches is strong enough to overcome mental laziness and the love of watching endless episodes of your favourite show on Netflix, and make them work.

The more clear and definite you make your picture then, and the more you dwell upon it, bringing out all its delightful details, the stronger your desire will be; and the stronger your desire, the easier it will be to hold your mind fixed upon the picture of what you want.

Something more is necessary, however, than merely to see the picture clearly. If that is all you do, you are only a dreamer, and will have little or no power for accomplishment.

Behind your clear vision must be the unwavering purpose to realise it; to actually do something about it.

And behind this purpose must be an invincible and unwavering KNOWLEDGE that the thing is already yours; that it is "at hand" out there in the Universe and you have only to move forwards and take possession of it.

Live in the new house, drive the new car, get on the plane's first class compartment, take your children to Disneyworld mentally, until it takes form around you physically. In the mental realm, enter at once into full enjoyment of the things you want. Feel it, hear it, smell it, touch it, taste it.

See the things you want as if they were actually around you all the time; see yourself as owning and using them. Make use of them in imagination just as you will use them when they are your tangible possessions.

Dwell upon your mental picture until it is clear and distinct, and then take the Mental Attitude of Ownership toward everything in that picture. Take possession of it, in your mind, in the full faith that it is actually yours. Hold to this mental ownership; do not waiver for an instant in the knowledge that it is real, it is just not quite in your current location.

And remember what was said in a proceeding chapter about gratitude; be as thankful for it all the time as you think about it as you expect to be when it has taken form and is in your current location.

The person who can sincerely thank Universal Energy for the things which as yet they own only in their imagination, has real faith, has real knowledge and power.

You will get rich; you will cause the creation of whatsoever you want.

You do not need to write it out or dream-board repeatedly for things you desire; it is not necessary to tell Universal Energy about it every day.

Your part is to intelligently formulate your desire for the things which make for a larger life, and to get these desires arranged into a coherent whole; and then to communicate this Whole Desire upon the Universal Energy, which has the power and the will to bring you what you want.

You do not make this impression by repeating strings of words; you make it by holding the vision with unshakable PURPOSE to attain it, and with steadfast KNOWLEDGE that you do attain it, that you are doing that right now.

The answers to becoming wealthy is not according to your knowledge while you are talking, but according to your knowledge while you are working.

You cannot impress the mind of Universal Energy by having a special day set apart to tell it what you want, and then forgetting it all during the rest of the week. You cannot communicate your desires by having special hours to go into your bathroom and ruminate, if you then dismiss the matter from your mind until the hour or day you have set aside comes again.

Affirmations are ok, and have their effect, especially upon you, in clarifying your vision and strengthening your knowledge; but it is not your affirmations which get you what you want.

In order to get rich you do not need a "sweet hour of affirmations"; you need to "affirm without ceasing." And by affirming I mean holding steadily to your vision, with the purpose to cause its creation into solid form, and the knowledge that you are doing so.

The whole success of the thing hinges on receiving, once you have clearly formed your vision.

When you have formed it, it is well to make an external statement of some kind, get it out of your head. A list, a vision board, creating a desktop background for your computer.

Once you have done that, from that moment on you must, in your mind, receive what you ask for.

Live in the new house; wear the fine clothes; ride in the Tesla; go on the journey, and confidently plan for greater journeys.

Think and speak to yourself in your mind of all the things you have asked for in terms of actual present ownership.

Imagine an environment, and a financial condition exactly as you want them, and live all the time – in your mind - in that imaginary environment and financial condition.

Mind out, however, that you do not do this as a day-dreamer and castle builder; hold to the KNOWLEDGE that the form of your desires are being realized, right now, out there somewhere and that now it's down to you to do to the ACTIONS that will enable you to receive them.

It is knowledge and purpose in the use of the imagination which make the difference between the scientist and the dreamer.

And having learned this fact, it is here that you must learn the proper use of the Will.

How to Use the Will

TO set about getting rich in a scientific way, you do not try to apply your will power to anything outside of yourself. You have no right to do so, anyway.

It is wrong to try and apply your will to other men and women, in order to get them to do what you want done.

It is as flagrantly wrong to coerce people by mental power as it is to coerce them by physical power.

You must avoid at all costs using skills like NLP or sales copywriting or hypnotic speaking from the stage to try and compel people to buy things that will not benefit them.

If compelling people by physical force to do things for you reduces them to slavery, compelling them by mental means accomplishes exactly the same thing; the only difference is in methods.

If taking things from people by physical force is robbery, them taking things by mental force is robbery also; there is no difference in principle.

You have no right to use your will power upon another person, even "for their own good"; for you do not know what is for their good.

You should not seek any control over other people, the only thing you should seek control over is how you REACT to them.

The science of getting rich does not require you to apply power or force to any other person, in any way whatsoever.

There is not the slightest necessity for doing so; indeed, any attempt to use your will upon others will only tend to defeat your purpose.

You do not need to apply your will to things, in order to compel them to come to you.

That would simply be trying to coerce Universal Energy, and would be foolish and useless, as well as counter productive.

You do not have to compel Universal Energy to give you good things, any more than you have to use your will power to make the sun rise, or to keep the plane you are flying in, in the sky. Those things are obeying natural laws.

The Building Blocks Of Life and Life Force is friendly to you, and is more anxious to give you what you want, than you are to get it. That is why, when you start down this path, good things happen to you more quickly than you ever imagined possible.

You were, quite literally standing in your own way.

To get rich, you need only to use your will power upon yourself.

When you know what to think and do, then you must use your will to compel yourself to think and do the right things. That is the legitimate use of the will in getting what you want - to use it in holding yourself to the right course. Use your will power to keep yourself thinking and acting in the Certain Way.

Do not try to project your will, or your thoughts, or your mind out into space, to "act" on things or people.

Keep your mind at home; it can accomplish more there than elsewhere.

Use your mind to form a mental image of what you want, and to hold that vision with knowledge and purpose; and use your will power to keep your mind working in the Right Way.

The more steady and continuous your knowledge and purpose, the more rapidly you will get rich, because you will make only POSITIVE impressions upon Universal Energy and the Building Blocks of Life; and you will not neutralise or offset them by negative thoughts or impressions.

This list or set of pictures of your desires, held by you in your mind and heart, with certain knowledge and purpose, making a positive impression and grateful vibrations is taken up by the Universal Energy, and permeates it – maybe to great distances throughout the universe, for all I know.

As this positive impression spreads, all things are set moving toward its realisation; every living thing, every inanimate thing, and the things yet uncreated, are stirred toward bringing into being that which you want.

All positive force begins to be exerted in that direction; all things begin to move toward you. Even the minds of people, everywhere, somehow are influenced toward doing the things necessary to the fulfilling of your desires; and they work for you, unconsciously.

People are certainly attracted by positive people on a mission, who don't bitch or complain about others, who don't give off vibes of neediness or lack of resourcefulness.

But you can stop all this in it's tracks, by starting up a negative impression in the Universal Energy.

Negativity or judgement of others, doubt or unbelief is as certain to start a negative movement away from you – to repel your desires - as knowledge and purpose are to start one toward you.

It is by not understanding this truth that most people who try to make use of "mental science" in getting rich fail.

Every hour and moment you spend in giving brain space to doubts and fears, every hour you spend in worry, every hour in which your soul is possessed by disbelief, sets a current away from you in the whole domain of Universal Energy.

Since belief – no, the certain knowledge that the things you desire can and will happen - is all important, you must get control and guard your thoughts; and as your knowledge will be shaped to a very great extent by the things you observe and think about daily, it is important that you should get control of your thoughts and be mindful of where you place your attention.

Don't go looking online for the forums where all the people there ever do is bitch about people who have become successful, like Salty Droid or the Warrior Forum.

These places do contain some great people, for sure, but also house many more negative people seeking to make themselves feel better about being unsuccessful.

There are many great positive and helpful groups to join, some free (like the "Internet Marketing Superfriends" or Yaro Starak's "Laptop Lifestyle" groups on Facebook) or for a small monthly charge (like my own at ClicksAndLeads.com or James Schramko's "Superfast Business" forum).

When I'm feeling low, I will listen to a positive podcast, or read a great book (like this one, or Synchronicity, or my friend Andy Shaw's Bug Free Mind books) to fill my mind with the right kind of positive thoughts and vibrations.

And here the will power comes into use; for it is by your will power that you determine what you will fix your attention on.

Remember, if you want to become rich, you must not make a study of poverty or spend all your time with poor people.

There's a popular quote about the total potential of your income being the average of the income's of the five people who you hang out with the most.

The poor do not need charity; they need inspiration.

Charity only sends them a loaf of bread to keep them alive in their wretchedness, or gives them an distraction to make them forget their misery for an hour or two; but inspiration will cause them to rise out of their misery. If you want to help the poor, demonstrate to them that they can become rich; prove it by getting rich yourself.

The only way in which poverty will ever be banished from this world is by getting a large and constantly increasing number of people to practice the teachings of this book.

People must be taught to become rich by creation, not by competition.

Everyone who becomes rich by competition kicks away the ladder by which he rises, and keeps others down; but every man who gets rich by creation opens a way for thousands to follow him, and inspires them to do so.

You are not showing hardness of heart or an unfeeling disposition when you refuse to pity poverty, see poverty, read about poverty, or think or talk about it, or to listen to those who do talk about it. Use your will power to keep your mind OFF the subject of poverty, and to keep it fixed with faith and purpose ON the vision of what you want.

Further Use of the Will

YOU cannot retain a true and clear vision of wealth if you are constantly turning your attention to opposing pictures, whether they be external or imaginary.

Do not retell the stories of your past troubles of a financial nature, if you have had them, do not think of them at all.

Do no tell of the poverty of your parents, or the hardships of your early life; to do any of these things is to mentally class yourself with the poor for the time being, and it will certainly check the movement of positive things in your direction.

Put poverty and all things that relate to poverty completely behind you.

You have accepted a certain theory of the universe as being correct, and are resting all your hopes of happiness on its being correct; and what can you gain by giving heed to conflicting theories?

Do not read books or watch videos on YouTube which tell you that the world is soon coming to an end, that we are all going to the devil.

The world is not going to the devil; it is going towards enlightenment. It is becoming more and more abundant all the time.

True, there may be a good many things in existing conditions which are disagreeable; but what is the use of spending all our time thinking about them when they are improving bit by bit, and when the study of them only tends to make us miserable and slow down our own progress (which will help and boost others) and keep them with us for longer?

Why give time and attention to things which are being removed by evolutionary growth and enlightenment, when you can hasten their removal only by promoting the evolutionary growth as far as your part of it goes?

No matter how horrible in seeming may be the conditions in certain countries, sections, or places, you waste your time and destroy your own chances by considering them.

You should interest yourself in the whole world's becoming rich.

Think of the riches the world is coming into, instead of the poverty it is growing out of; and bear in mind that the only way in which you can assist the world in growing rich is by growing rich yourself through the creative method, but not the competitive one.

Give your attention wholly to riches; ignore poverty.

Whenever you think or speak of those who are poor, think and speak of them as those who are becoming rich; as those who are to be congratulated rather than pitied. Then they, and others around you both will catch the inspiration, and begin to search for the way out.

Because I say that you are to give your whole time and mind and thought to riches, it does not follow that you are to be sordid or mean.

To become really rich is the noblest aim you can have in life, for it includes everything else.

On the competitive level, the struggle to get rich is a scramble for power over other men; but when we come into the creative mindset, all this is changed.

Everyone always marvels at the way we all, in internet marketing, get together at Conferences and Masterminds and freely share our knowledge and skills, what's working for us right now.

We don't need to be competitive; there so SO MANY ways to make money online, we don't need to fight and scramble for the scraps. There are more people coming online all the time who want to know what we know, more than we could ever serve singly!

All that is possible in the creative mindset and collaborative spirit is the way of greatness and soul fulfilment, of service and honest endeavor, this all comes by way of getting rich; all is made possible by the free use of things, many things.

If you lack for physical health, you will find that the attainment of it is only helped by your getting rich.

Only those who are emancipated from financial worry, and who have the means to live a care-free, stress-free life, sleep well, exercise and buy the supplements they need and organic food that nourishes them can have, and retain good health.

Moral and spiritual greatness is possible only to those who are above the competitive battle for existence; and only those who are becoming rich on the plane of creative thought are free from the degrading influences of competition.

If your heart is set on domestic happiness, remember that love flourishes best where there is love, support and a nurturing environment; and these are to be found only where riches are attained by the exercise of creative thought, without strife or rivalry.

You can aim at nothing so great and admirable, I repeat, as to become rich; and you must fix your attention upon your mental picture of riches, to the exclusion of all that may tend to dim or obscure the vision.

You must learn to see the underlying TRUTH in all things; you must see, beneath all seemingly wrong conditions, the Universal Energy and Life Force ever moving forward toward fuller expression and more complete happiness.

It is the truth that there is no such thing as poverty; that there is only wealth.

Some people remain in poverty because they are ignorant of the fact that there is wealth for them; and these can best be taught by showing them the way to affluence in your own person and practice.

Others are poor because, while they feel that there might be a way out, they are too damn lazy to put forth the mental effort necessary to find that way and by travel it; and for these the very best thing you can do is to arouse their desire to do the same by showing them the happiness that comes from being rightly rich.

Others still are poor because, while they have some notion of science, they have become so swamped and lost in the maze of business models, strategies, tactics, tools and tricks that they do not know which road to take.

They try a mixture of many systems, pay many "gurus" and still fail in all. For these people , again, the very best thing, to do is to show the right way in your own person and practice; an ounce of doing things is worth a pound of theorising and spouting forth from the stage.

The very best thing you can do for the whole world is to make the most of yourself.

You can serve Universal Energy, yourself and your fellow man in no more effective way than by getting rich.

Another thing. We assert that this book gives in detail the principles of the science of getting rich; and if that is true, you do not need to read any other book upon the subject.

This may sound narrow and egotistical, but remember: there is no more scientific method of computation in mathematics than by addition, subtraction, multiplication, and division; no other method is possible.

There can be but one shortest distance between two points.

It's exactly the same in internet marketing. It's a simple science with a bit of maths thrown in, which goes as follows:

The most direct method, the shortest difference between two points, is placing an advertisement on a page, with a hopefully compelling offer on, taking the potential customer to a sales page with a link to a checkout online.

If that doesn't work, you might place one more step in between, that of advertising a free gift which requires a visit to a landing page, or to a value filled blog post with an optin box on it.

Then, you might show your 2nd ad to the people who visited the landing page or the blog post but who didn't put their name and email in the box to get the free gift.

You follow up with those who clicked but didn't optin in a certain way, you follow up with those who did optin, but then didn't buy, in another.

If someone bought your product or service, you offer them something else, something that compliments the first product or service.

If the person bought one offer but not the next, you might offer them something else, something that is tangential to the first product.

Back to the maths....

Your goal is to acquire a new customer for less than the amount of the profit you are willing to give up, to aquire the customer.

Most online businesses know that they won't make a profit on the first purchase, but they also know how much a customer is worth to them in profit over the first 2-3 purchases, or over the first year, for example.

It's no more complicated that that, to make money online, albeit that there are quite a few tools you can use to achieve the above goals.

Your job is to set out your suite of products or services and get in front of as large a "hungry crowd" as possible and then hone each part of your marketing and product funnel as possible, by means of tracking progress through that funnel.

If you improve each part of a 10-step funnel by just 10%, you don't improve your results by 100% but by 1000%.

So why is it so hard for most people to do?

Because they don't know, deep in their hearts that they will succeed.

They don't determine that they will use their will to overcome obstacles, learn the skills and attract those they need to them. They stop thinking scientifically and start thinking emotionally.

There is only one way to think scientifically, and that is to think in the way that leads by the most direct and simple route to the goal.

No one has yet formulated a briefer or less complex "system" for wealth creation than the one set forth in this book; it has been stripped of all non-essentials.

When you start today, with this book, lay all others aside; put them out of your mind altogether.

Read this book every day; keep it with you; commit it to memory, and do not think about other "systems" and theories.

If you do, you will begin to have doubts, and to be uncertain and wavering in your thought; and then you will begin to fail and then attract negative things to happen to you.

After you have made your first dollars online and then become rich, you may study other systems as much as you please; but until you are quite sure that you have achieved what you want, do not read anything on this line but this book, unless it be the authors mentioned in the Preface.

And read only the most optimistic comments on the world's news; those in harmony with your picture.

Remember!

There are Building Blocks Of Life and a Life Force from which all things are made, and which, permeates, penetrates, and fills the interspaces of the universe.

In order to do this, we must pass from the competitive to the creative mind; we must form a clear mental picture of the things we desire, and not only express those desires in a physical form, like a list or set of pictures, we hold this picture in our thoughts with the fixed PURPOSE to get what we desire, and the unwavering KNOWLEDGE that we will get what we desire, closing our mind against all that may tend to shake our purpose, dim our vision, or quench our certain knowledge that this is happening right now.

And in addition to all this, we shall now see that we must live and act in a Certain Way.

Acting in the Certain Way

THOUGHT is the creative power, or the impelling force which causes the creative power to act; thinking in a Certain Way will bring riches to you, but you must not rely upon thought alone, paying no attention to personal action.

That is the rock upon which many otherwise scientific metaphysical thinkers meet shipwreck, the failure to connect thought with personal action.

This is the bit that was largely missed by most viewers of the 2006 film "The Secret".

While 3D Printers are boggling the minds of all who see them at work, we have not yet reached the stage of development, in which people can create directly from the Building Blocks Of Life without either the support of nature's processes or the work of human hands; we must not only think, but our personal action must add to and support our thoughts.

By thought you can cause the gold in the hearts of the mountains to be impelled toward you; but it will not mine itself, refine itself, coin itself into double eagles, print itself onto dollar bills and come rolling and fluttering along the roads seeking its way into your pocket.

Under the impelling power of the Universal Energy, men's affairs will be arranged that some one will be led to mine the gold for you; other men's business transactions will be so directed that the gold will be brought toward you, and you must so arrange your own business affairs that you may be able to receive it when it comes to you.

Your thought makes all things, animate and inanimate, work to bring you what you want; but your personal activity must be such that you can rightly receive what you want when it reaches you. You are not to take it as charity, nor to steal it; you must give every man more in use value than he gives you in cash value.

The scientific use of thought consists in forming a clear and distinct mental image of what you desire; in holding fast to the purpose to get what you desire; and in realising with grateful knowledge that you do get what you desire.

The action of thought in getting rich is fully explained in the preceding chapters; your faith and purpose positively impress your vision upon the Building Blocks Of Life and the Life Force, both of which has the same desire for more life that you have; and this vision, received from you, sets all the creative forces at work in and through their regular channels of action, but directed toward you.

It is not your part to guide or supervise the creative process; all you have to do with that is to retain your vision, stick to your purpose, and maintain your faith and gratitude.

But you must act in a Certain Way, so that you can take legally what is yours when it comes to you; so that you can meet the things you have in your picture, and put them in their proper places as they arrive.

You can really see the truth of this. When things reach you, they will be in the hands of other men, who will ask an equivalent exchange of energy for them.

And you can only get what is yours by giving the other man what is his.

Your pocketbook is not going to be transformed into old Fortunate's purse, which shall be always full of money without any effort on your part.

This is the crucial point in the science of getting rich; right here, where thought and personal action must be combined.

There are very many people who, consciously or unconsciously, set the creative forces in action by the strength and persistence of their desires, but who remain poor because they do not provide for the reception of the thing they want when it comes.

By thought, the thing you desire is brought to you; by action you receive it.

Whatever your action is to be, it is evident that you must act NOW.

You cannot act in the past, and it is essential to the clearness of your mental vision that you dismiss the past from your mind.

You cannot act in the future, for the future is not here yet.

And you cannot tell how you will want to act in any future situation until that situation has arrived.

Because you are not in the right business, or the right environment now, do not think that you must postpone action until you get into the right business or environment.

And do not spend time in the present thinking and worrying as to the best course in possible future emergencies; have faith in your ability to meet any emergency when it arrives.

If you act in the present with your mind on the future, your present action will be with a divided mind, and will not be effective.

Put your whole mind into present action.

Do not give your creative impulse to Universal Energy and then sit down and wait for results; if you do, you will never get them.

Act now.

There is never any time but now, and there never will be any time but now. If you are ever to begin to make ready for the reception of what you want, you must begin now.

And your action, whatever it is, must most likely be in your present business or employment, and must be upon the persons and things in your present environment.

You cannot act where you are not; you cannot act where you have been, and you cannot act where you are going to be; you can act only where you are.

Do not bother as to whether yesterday's work was well done or ill done; do today's work well.

Even if you have failed in the past, start again to the best of your ability and to the best use of the tools and knowledge that you have available. You are a different person now.

Do not try to do tomorrow's work now; there will be plenty of time to do that when you get to it. By creating a 10 year, 3 year, 1 year, 90 day plan you can do as much as you need to do without getting overwhelmed and burning out.

Do not try, by means of so-called biz opp, biz-in-a-box or magic buttons to bypass the elementary and essential steps needed to build a successful business online.

Do not wait for a change of environment, before you act; get a change of environment by action.

Do not worry about the fact that you don't know how to use or can't afford the "best of breed" tools, find the best and the least expensive way forwards and know that you can always upgrade later.

Look around you, see what you are tolerating in your environment that is distracting you or making you feel poor or unsupported. You can act positively upon the environment in which you are now, in small ways, as to cause yourself to be working in or transferred to a better environment.

Hold with certain knowledge and purpose the vision of yourself in the better environment, but act upon your present environment with all your heart, and with all your strength, and with all your mind.

Do not spend any time in day dreaming or castle building; hold to the one vision of what you want, and act NOW.

Do not cast about seeking some new thing to do, or some strange, unusual, or remarkable action to perform as a first step toward getting rich.

It is probable that your actions, at least for some time to come, will be those you have been performing for some time past; but you are to begin now to perform these actions in the Certain Way, which will surely make you rich.

If you are engaged in some business, and feel that it is not the right one for you, do not wait until you get into the right business before you begin to act.

If you are in employment and it's not the area you want to work in forever, start a part time business online or offline, outside the hours of your job, to move you towards the area that you do want to be working in.

Do not feel discouraged, or sit down and moan to your co-workers because you are misplaced. No one was ever so misplaced but that he could not find the right place, and no-one ever became so involved in the wrong business but that he could get into the right business.

Hold the vision of yourself in the right business, with the purpose to get into it, and the faith that you will get into it, and are getting into it; but ACT in your present business.

Use your present business as the stepping stone or means of getting a better one, and use your present environment as the means of getting into a better one.

Your vision of the right business, if held with faith and purpose, will cause the Universe to move the right business toward you; and your actions, if performed in the Certain Way, will cause you to move toward the business.

If you are an employee, or wage earner, and feel that you must change places in order to get what you want, do not 'project" your thought into space and rely upon it to get you another job. It will probably fail to do so.

Hold the clear vision of yourself in the job you want, while you ACT with faith and purpose on the job you have, and you will certainly find doors starting to open for you and people starting to appear who can help and mentor you.

Your vision and faith will set the creative force in motion to bring it toward you, and your action will cause the forces in your own environment to move you toward the place you want.

In closing this chapter, we will add another statement to our syllabus:--

There are Building Blocks Of Life and a Life Force from which all things are made, and which, permeates, penetrates, and fills the interspaces of the universe.

In order to do this, we must pass from the competitive to the creative mind; we must form a clear mental picture of the things we desire, and not only express those desires in a physical form, like a list or set of pictures, we hold this picture in our thoughts with the fixed PURPOSE to get what we desire, and the unwavering KNOWLEDGE that we will get what we desire.

We must close our mind against all that may tend to shake our purpose, dim our vision, or quench our certain knowledge that this is happening and moving towards us right now.

That we may receive what we desire when it comes, we must act NOW positively upon the people and things in our present environment.

We must make the best of and use the environments and tools at our disposal now, knowing that we can always upgrade later and even if we don't know how to do something now, we will soon acquire the knowledge, skills or team members we need to achieve that thing.

Efficient Action

You must use your thought as directed in previous chapters, and begin to do what you can do, where you are; and you must do ALL that you can do, where you are.

In other words, it's not just about taking some action, but not just any old action, massive action, more action than you initially think you'll need.

You can advance and attract abundance only be "being larger" than your current place; and no-one is ever larger than their present place who doesn't do any of the work that is necessary for that place.

The world is advanced and made more abundant only by those who MORE than fill their present places.

If nobody quite filled his present place, you can see that there must be a going backward in everything. Those who do not quite fill their present places are dead weight upon society, government, commerce, and industry; they must be carried along by others at a great expense.

The progress of the world is held back only by those who do not fill the places they are holding; they belong to a former age and a lower stage or plane of life, and their tendency is toward degeneration.

No society could advance if every man was smaller than his place; social evolution is guided by the law of physical and mental evolution.

In the animal world, evolution is caused by an excess of life.

When an organism has more life than can be expressed in the functions of its own plane, it develops the organs of a higher plane, and a new species is originated.

There never would have been new species had there not been organisms which more than filled their places. The law is exactly the same for you; your getting rich depends upon your applying this principle to your own affairs.

Every day is either a successful day (a day in which you have more than filled your place) or a day of failure (a day in which you have not completely filled your place); and it is the successful days which get you what you want.

If every day is a failure, you can never get rich; while if every day is a success, you cannot fail to get rich.

If there is something that may be done today, and you do not do it, you have failed in so far as that thing is concerned; and the consequences may be more disastrous than you imagine.

There will be an "opportunity cost" to the things that you have not yet done. Things that would have happened as a result of those things, will not now happen. Everything you do sets into work forces that move on your behalf.

You cannot foresee the results of even the most trivial act; you do not yet know the workings of all the forces that have been set moving in your behalf. Much may be depending on your doing some simple act; it may be the very thing, the VERY THING which is to open the door of opportunity to very great possibilities.

The founder of Apple, Steve Jobs, explained this in his Commencement Speech at Stanford University by saying:

"You can't connect the dots looking forward; you can only connect them looking backwards. So you have to trust that the dots will somehow connect in your future."

Your actions are your dots.

The Time/Space Continuum theory of physics says that, at any given moment, there are infinite versions of what is happening right now, happening over many different universes.

So it follows that each act you take or don't' take, may change the infinite variety of possibilities for the next moment and the next and next month and next year.

One action taken here, one not taken there, may change your future for ever, you can easily see that now.

You can never know all the combinations which Universal Energy is making for you in the world of things and of things and of human affairs; your neglect or failure to do some small thing may ultimately cause a long delay in getting what you want.

Do, every day, ALL that can be done that day.

There is, however, a limitation or qualification of the above that you must take into account.

You are not to overwork, nor to rush blindly into your business in the effort to do the greatest possible number of things in the shortest possible time.

You are not to try to do tomorrow's work today, nor to do a week's work in a day. That way lies total burnout.

This is why it's so important to make (and then keep re-making) your 10 year, 3 year, 1 year, 90 day, 30 day, 7 day plans and to keep track on a weekly basis of whether you are on track to make those plans happen, even if the day to day tasks to achieve those goals (and even those goals) may change regularly.

When my friend Steve died in March, I completely changed my long term goals because I felt completely different about life.

(My Mastermind groups are specifically designed to help people formulate their plans and then to keep track of whether they are staying on track for their plans, without burnout. If you would like to find out about those, visit https://NicolaCairncross.com/mastermind or just get onto my email list and keep opening my emails)

It is really not the number of things you do, but the EFFICIENCY of each separate action that counts.

Every act is, in itself, either a success or a failure. Every act is, in itself, either effective or inefficient.

Every inefficient act is a failure, and if you spend your life in doing inefficient acts, your whole life will be a failure.

The more things you do, the worse for you, if all your acts are inefficient ones.

On the other hand, every efficient act is a success in itself, and if every act of your life is an efficient one, your whole life MUST be a success.

The cause of failure is doing too many things in an inefficient manner, and not doing enough things in an efficient manner.

You will see that it is a self-evident proposition that if you do not do any inefficient acts, and if you do a sufficient number of efficient acts, you will become rich.

If, now, it is possible for you to make each act an efficient one, you see again that the getting of riches is reduced to an exact science, like mathematics.

The matter turns, then, on the question whether you can make each separate act a success in itself. And this you can certainly do.

You can make each act a success, because Universal Energy is working with you; and Universal Energy cannot fail.

Power is at your service; and to make each act efficient you have only to put power into it.

Every action is either strong or weak; and when every one is strong, you are acting in the Certain Way which will make you rich.

Every act can be made strong and efficient by holding your vision while you are doing it, and putting the whole power of your KNOWLEDGE OF SUCCESS and PURPOSE into it.

Warning: It is at this point that the people fail who separate mental power from personal action.

They use the power of mind in one place and at one time, and they act in another pace and at another time.

So their acts are not successful in themselves; too many of them are inefficient.

But if Universal Energy goes into every act, no matter how commonplace, every act will be a success in itself; and as in the nature of things every success opens the way to other successes, your progress toward what you want, and the progress of what you want toward you, will become increasingly rapid.

Remember that successful action is cumulative in its results. We are talking about the power of compound interest here, where 10 turns into 20, into 40, into 80, into 160, into 320, into 640, into 1280 etc.

Einstein described compound interest at "the 8th Wonder of the world" and you can put that to work for you.

Since the desire for more life is inherent in all things, when a man begins to move toward a larger life more things attach themselves to him, more people are attracted to his cause and the influence of his desire is multiplied.

Do, every day, all that you can do that day, and do each act in an efficient manner.

In saying that you must hold your vision while you are doing each act, however trivial or commonplace, I do not mean to say that it is necessary at all times to see the vision distinctly to its smallest details.

It should be the work of your leisure hours to use your imagination on the details of your vision, and to contemplate them until they are firmly fixed upon memory. If you wish speedy results, spend practically all your spare time in this practice.

By continuous contemplation you will get the picture of what you want, even to the smallest details, so firmly fixed upon your mind, and so completely transferred to the "mind" of The Building Blocks Of Life, that in your working hours you need only to mentally refer to the picture to stimulate your faith and purpose, and cause your best effort to be put forth.

Contemplate your picture in your leisure hours until your consciousness is so full of it that you can grasp it instantly. You will become so enthused with its bright promises that the mere thought of it will call forth the strongest energies of your whole being.

(As I was thinking about re-writing this book after having re-read it, I kept getting waves of excitement come over me, I literally kept getting tingles down my neck and I could NOT WAIT to get to the computer to continue this work, which does not feel like work at all by the way!)

Let us again repeat our syllabus, and by slightly changing the closing statements bring it to the point we have now reached.

There are Building Blocks Of Life and a Life Force from which all things are made, and which, permeates, penetrates, and fills the interspaces of the universe.

We must form a clear mental picture of the things we desire, and not only express those desires in a physical form, like a list or set of pictures, we must hold this picture in our thoughts with the fixed PURPOSE to get what we desire, and the unwavering KNOWLEDGE that we will get what we desire.

We must close our mind against all that may tend to shake our purpose, dim our vision, or quench our certain knowledge that this is happening and moving towards us right now.

That we may receive what we desire when it comes, we must act NOW positively upon the people and things in our present environment.

We must make the best of and use the environments and tools at our disposal now, knowing that we can always upgrade later and even if we don't know how to do something now, we will soon acquire the knowledge, skills or team members we need to achieve that thing.

In order to do this, we must pass from the competitive to the creative mind; we must form a clear mental picture of the things we want, and do, with faith and purpose, all of the thing that can be done each day, doing each separate thing in an efficient manner.

Getting into the Right Business

Success, in any particular business, depends for one thing upon your possessing in a well-developed state the talent, knowledge and skills required in that business.

Some businesses need raw talent, but many do not, as the knowledge and skills can be acquired or bought.

Without good musical talent no one can succeed as a performer or teacher of music; without well-developed mechanical faculties no one can achieve great success in any of the mechanical trades; without tact and a knowledge of how people work, no one can succeed in business pursuits.

But to possess in a well-developed state the talent required in your particular vocation does not insure getting rich.

There are musicians who have remarkable talent, and who yet remain poor; there are blacksmiths, carpenters, and so on who have excellent mechanical ability, but who do not get rich; and there are merchants with good faculties for dealing with other people who nevertheless fail.

The different faculties are tools; it is essential to have good tools, but it is also essential that the tools should be used in the Right Way.

One man can take a sharp saw, a square, a good plane, and so on, and build a handsome article of furniture; another man can take the same tools and set to work to duplicate the article, but his production will be a botch. He does not know how to use good tools in a successful way.

The various faculties of your mind are the tools with which you must do the work which is to make you rich; it will be easier for you to succeed if you get into a business for which you are well equipped with mental tools.

You can discover the tools that your mind naturally provides and where you are naturally most strong in, by doing a couple of psychological tests online. Two of the best known which I recommend and use to work with my clients are the Wealth Dynamics test, by Roger Hamilton, the Kolbe A test by the Kolbe Institute.

Generally speaking, you will do best in that business which will use your strongest faculties; the one for which you are naturally "best fitted." But there are limitations to this statement, also. No one should regard their vocation as being irrevocably fixed by the tendencies with which they were born.

You can get rich in ANY business, for if you have not the right talent for you can develop that talent; it merely means that you will have to make your tools as you go along, instead of confining yourself to the use of those with which you were born.

It will be EASIER for you to succeed in a business arena for which you already have the talents in a well-developed state; but you CAN succeed in any vocation, for you can develop any rudimentary talent, and there is no talent of which you have not at least the rudiment.

You will get rich most easily in point of effort, if you do that for which you are best fitted; but you will get rich most satisfactorily if you do that which you WANT to do.

Doing what you want to do is life; and there is no real satisfaction in living if we are compelled to be forever doing something which we do not like to do, and if we can never do what we want to do.

And it is certain that you CAN do what you want to do; the desire to do it is proof that you have within you the power which can do it.

Desire is a manifestation of power.

The desire to play music is the power which can play music seeking expression and development; the desire to invent mechanical devices is the mechanical talent seeking expression and development.

My desire to write the three books that went before this one, and now to re-write this book, is the power to take ideas and express them in words seeking expression and development. I must say, when I get inspired to write, it always feels like it's coming through me, not from me.

It also feels like it can't be denied, not for long and certainly not at all!

Where there is no power, either developed or undeveloped, to do a thing, there is never any desire to do that thing; and where there is strong desire to do a thing, it is certain proof that the power to do it is strong, and only requires to be developed and applied in the Right Way.

All things else being equal, it is best to select the business for which you have the best developed talent; but if you have a strong desire to engage in any particular line of work, you should select that work as the ultimate end at which you aim.

You can do what you want to do, and it is your right and privilege to follow the business or vocation which will be most congenial and pleasant.

You are not obliged to do what you do not like to do, and should not do it except as a means to bring you to the doing of the thing you want to do.

If there are past mistakes whose consequences have placed you in an undesirable business or environment, you may be obliged for some time to do what you do not like to do; but you can make the doing of it pleasant by knowing that it is making it possible for you to come to the doing of what you want to do.

If you feel that you are not in the right vocation, do not act too hastily in trying to get into another one. Do not leap from the frying pan into the fire!

The best way, generally, to change your business or environment is by growth.

Do not be afraid to make a sudden and radical change if the opportunity is presented, and you feel after careful consideration that it is the right opportunity; but never take sudden or radical action when you are in doubt as to the wisdom of doing so.

There is never any hurry on the creative plane; and there is no lack of opportunity.

When you get out of the competitive mind you will understand that you never need to act hastily. No one else is going to beat you to the thing you want to do; there is enough for all.

If one space is taken, another and a better one will be opened for you a little farther on; there is plenty of time.

When you are in doubt, wait.

Fall back on the contemplation of your vision, and increase your faith and purpose; and by all means, in times of doubt and indecision, cultivate gratitude.

A day or two spent in contemplating the vision of what you desire, and in feeling thankful and holding the absolute and certain knowledge that you are getting your desire, it's on it's way, enjoying feeling the happiness and gratitude for that, that will bring your mind into such close relationship with the Universal Energy that you will make no mistake when you do act.

Mistakes come from acting hastily, or from acting in fear or doubt, or in forgetfulness of the Right Motive, which is to create more life to all, and less to none.

As you go on in the Certain Way, opportunities will come to you in increasing number; and you will need to be very steady in your faith and purpose, and to keep in close touch with Universal Energy by the act of feeling gratitude.

Do all that you can do in a perfect manner every day, but do it without haste, worry, or fear. Go as fast as you can, but never hurry.

Remember that in the moment you begin to hurry you cease to be a creator and become a competitor; you drop back upon the old plane again.

Whenever you find yourself hurrying or even feelling the need to hurry, call a halt; fix your attention on the mental image of the thing you desire, and begin to give thanks that you are getting it.

The exercise of GRATITUDE will never fail to strengthen your certain knowledge of success and renew your purpose.

The Impression of Increase

WHETHER you change your vocation or business or not, your actions for the present must be those pertaining to the business in which you are now engaged.

You can get into the business you want by making constructive use of the business you are already established in; by doing your daily work in a Certain Way.

And in so far as your business consists in dealing with other people, whether personally or online, the key-thought of all your efforts must be to convey to their minds the impression of increase and abundance.

Increase and abundance is what everyone is seeking; it is the urge of the Universal Energy within them, seeking fuller expression.

The desire for abundance is inherent in all nature; it is the fundamental impulse of the universe. All human activities are based on the desire for more; people are seeking more food, more clothes, better shelter, more luxury, more beauty, more knowledge, more pleasure – the increase in something, more life.

Every living thing is under this necessity for continuous advancement; where something is not growing, it's dying.

Mankind instinctively knows this, and hence we are forever seeking more.

The normal desire for increased wealth is not an evil or a reprehensible thing; it is simply the desire for more abundant life; it is aspiration.

And because it is the deepest instinct of their natures, everyone is attracted to that person who can give them more of the means of life.

In following the Certain Way as described in the foregoing pages, you are creating a continuous increase of abundance for yourself, and you are giving it to all with whom you come into contact.

You are a creative centre, from which the opportunity for increase and abundance is given off to all.

Be sure of this, and convey assurance of the fact to every man, woman, and child with whom you come in contact.

No matter how small the transaction, even if it be only the selling of a stick of candy to the mother of a little child, do everything you can to put into it the thought of abundance, and make sure that the customer is left with that impression.

Convey the impression of advancement with everything you do, so that everyone you come into contact with shall receive the impression that you are an Abundant Person, and that you help all who deal with you.

Even to the people whom you meet in a social way, without any thought of business, and to whom you do not try to sell anything, give the thought of increase and abundance.

You can convey this impression by holding the unshakable faith that you, yourself, are in the Way of Increase & Abundance; and by letting this knowledge inspire, fill, and permeate every action.

Do everything that you do in the firm conviction that you are an increasing and abundant personality, and that you are giving that help and feeling to everybody.

Feel, no, KNOW that you are getting rich, and that in so doing you are making others rich, and that you will be conferring benefits (of all kind, not money necessarily) on all.

Do not boast or brag of your success, or talk about it unnecessarily; true, deep knowledge of certain success is never boastful. Wherever you find a boastful person, you find one who is secretly doubtful and afraid.

Simply feel the true, deep knowledge, and let it work out in every transaction; let every act and tone and look express the quiet assurance that you are getting rich; that you are already rich. Words will not be necessary to communicate this feeling to others; they will feel the sense of increase and abundance when in your presence, and will be attracted to you again.

You must so impress others that they will feel that in associating with you some of that true, deep knowledge will rub off.

See that, in every transaction, you give them a use value greater than the cash value you are taking from them.

Take an honest pride in doing this, and let everybody know it; and you will have no lack of customers.

People will go where they are given increase and abundance; and Universal Energy, which desires increase in all, and which knows all, will move toward you men and women who have never heard of you.

Your business will increase rapidly, and you will be surprised at the unexpected benefits which will come to you.

You will be able, from day to day to make larger combinations, secure greater advantages, and to go on into a more congenial vocation or business if you desire to do so.

But doing thing all this, you must never lose sight of your vision of what you desire, or your true, deep knowledge and purpose to get what you want.

Let me here give you another word of caution in regard to motives.

Beware of the insidious temptation to seek for power over other people.

Nothing is so pleasant to the unformed or only partially developed mind as the exercise of power or dominion over others. The desire to rule for selfish gratification has been the curse of the world. For countless ages kings and lords have drenched the earth with blood in their battles to extend their dominions; this not to seek more life for all, but to get more power for themselves.

To-day, as we have seen with the recent global financial collapse of 2008 / 2009, the main motive in the business and industrial world is the same; people marshal their armies of dollars, and lay waste the lives and hearts of millions in the same mad scramble for power over others. Commercial kings, like political kings, are inspired by the lust of money and for power.

Look out for the temptation to seek for authority, to become a "master," to be considered as one who is above normal people, to impress others by lavish display, and so on.

The mind that seeks for mastery over others is the competitive mind; and the competitive mind is not the creative one.

In order to master your environment and your destiny, it is not at all necessary that you should rule over your fellow men and indeed, when you fall into the world's struggle for the high places, you begin to be conquered by fate and environment, and your getting rich becomes a matter of chance and speculation.

Beware of the competitive mind!! No better statement of the principle of creative action can be formulated than the favourite declaration of the late Sam "Golden Rule" Jones of Toledo: "What I want for myself, I want for everybody."

(Samuel Milton "Golden Rule" Jones (1846 - 1904) was a forward thinking Mayor of Toledo, Ohio from 1897 to until the time of his death in 1904. Jones was famous for his outspoken advocacy of the proverbial ethic of reciprocity or "Golden Rule," hence his nickname. Read more about Mr Jones here)

The Advancing Person

WHAT I have said in the last chapter applies as well to the professional person (doctors, lawyers, accountants) and the average wage-earner as to the person who is engaged in business.

No matter whether you are a physician, a teacher, or a lawyer, if you can give increase of life and abundance of thought or action to others and make them feel that, they will be attracted to you, and you will get rich.

The doctor who holds the vision of himself as a great and successful healer, and who works toward the complete realisation of that vision with true, deep knowledge and purpose, as described in former chapters, will come into such close touch with Universal Energy and the Life Force that he will be phenomenally successful; patients will come to him in throngs.

The combined mental and personal action I have described is infallible; it cannot fail.

Everyone who follows these instructions steadily, perseveringly, and to the letter, will get rich. The law of the Increase of Life is as mathematically certain in its operation as the law of gravitation; getting rich is an exact science.

The averagely employed person will find this as true of his case as of any of the others mentioned.

Do not feel that you have no chance to get rich because you are working where there is no visible opportunity for advancement, where wages are small and the cost of living high. Form your clear mental vision of what you want, and begin to act with faith and purpose.

Do all the work you can do, every day, and do each piece of work in a perfectly successful manner; put the power of success, and the purpose to get rich, into everything that you do.

But do not do this merely with the idea of ingratiating yourself with your employer, in the hope that he, or those above you, will see your good work and advance you; it is not likely that they will do so.

The person who is merely "good" at their job, filling their place to the very best of their ability, and satisfied with that, is valuable to his employer; and it is not to the employer's interest to promote that person; he is worth more where he is.

Even more so when someone is MORE than filling their place! What a bargain that employer is getting then!

No, to secure advancement, something more is necessary than just to be too large for your current place.

The person who is certain to advance is the one who is too big for his place AND who has a clear concept of what they want to be; who knows that they can become what they want to be and who is determined to BE what you want to be.

Do not try to more than fill your present place with a view to pleasing your employer; do it with the idea of advancing yourself.

Think of it as you practicing every day now to be the person that you will need to be later.

Hold the deep and certain knowledge of success and the concept of increase and abundance during work hours, after work hours, and before work hours.

Hold it in such a way that every person who comes in contact with you, whether foreman, fellow workman, or social acquaintance, will feel the power of purpose radiating from you; so that every one will get the sense of advancement and increase from you.

Everyone will be attracted to you, in an energetic way, and if there is no possibility for advancement in your present job, you will very soon see an opportunity to take another job.

There is a Universal Energy which never fails to present opportunity to the Advancing Man who is moving in obedience to law.

Universal Energy and Life Force cannot help helping you, if you act in a Certain Way; it must do so in order to help itself for that is the way of the Universe.

There is nothing in your circumstances or in the economic situation that can keep you down.

If you cannot get rich working in one business arena, you can move your talent, knowledge and skills to another business arena; and if you begin to move in the Certain Way, you will certainly escape from the "clutches" of the dying business arena you may be in now, and get into the new business arena or wherever else you wish to be.

Business Owners can only keep people in so-called hopeless conditions only so long as there are people who are too ignorant to know of the science of getting rich, or if they know about it, are just too damn lazy to practice it.

Begin this way of thinking and acting, and your deep knowledge and purpose will make you quick to see any opportunity to better your condition.

Such opportunities will speedily come, for Universal Energy and Life Force, working in all things, and working for you, will bring them before you.

Do not wait for an opportunity to be all that you want to be; when an opportunity to be more than you are now is presented, and you feel impelled toward it, take it. It will be the first step toward a greater opportunity.

There is no such thing possible in this universe as a lack of opportunities for the person who is living the advancing life.

It is inherent in the constitution of the cosmos that all things shall be for you and work together for your good; and you will certainly get rich if you act and think in the Certain Way.

So let any person, no matter what your current work circumstances study this book with great care, and enter with confidence upon the course of action it prescribes; it will not fail you.

A Few Warnings & Concluding Observations

MANY people will laugh at the idea that there is an exact science of getting rich; holding the impression that the supply of wealth is limited, they will insist that social and governmental institutions must be changed before even any considerable number of people can acquire abundance.

But this is not true.

It is true that existing governments "keep" the masses in poverty, by not teaching these methods in schools, but this is also because most people do not naturally think and act in the Certain Way.

If most people begin to move forward as suggested in this book, neither governments nor industrial systems can stop them or keep them down; all systems must be modified to accommodate the forward movement.

If most people had the Advancing Mind, have the deep knowledge in their minds and hearts that they can become rich, and move forward with the fixed purpose to become rich, nothing can possibly keep them in poverty.

Individuals may enter upon the Certain Way at any time, and under any government, and make themselves rich; and when any considerable number of individuals do so under any government, they will naturally be included in the system and cause the system to be changed as to open the way for others.

The more people who get rich on the competitive plane, the worse for others; the more people who get rich on the creative plane, the better for others.

The economic salvation of everyone else can only be accomplished by encouraging a large number of people to practice the scientific method set down in this book, and become rich.

These will show others the way, and inspire them with a desire for real life, with the faith that it can be attained, and with the purpose to attain it.

For the present, however, it is enough to know that neither the government under which you live nor the capitalistic or competitive system of industry can keep you from getting rich.

When you enter upon the creative plane of thought you will rise above all these things and become a citizen of another kingdom altogether.

But remember that your thought must be held upon the creative plane; you are never for an instant to be betrayed into regarding the supply as limited, or into acting in the spirit of competition.

Whenever you do fall into your old ways of thought, correct yourself instantly; for when you are in the competitive mind, you have lost the cooperation of Universal Energy and the Life Force that flows through us all.

Do not spend any time in worrying and planning as to how you will meet possible emergencies in the future, except as the necessary policies may affect your actions today.

You are just to be concerned with doing today's work in a perfectly successful manner, and not with emergencies which may arise tomorrow; you can attend to them as they come.

Do not concern yourself with questions as to how you shall surmount future obstacles which may loom upon your business horizon, unless you can see plainly that your course must be altered today in order to avoid them.

No matter how tremendous an obstruction may appear at a distance, you will find that if you go on in the Certain Way it will disappear as you approach it, or that a way over, though, or around it will appear.

No possible combination of circumstances can defeat someone who is proceeding to get rich along strictly scientific lines. No-one who obeys the law can fail to get rich, any more than one can multiply two by two and fail to get four.

Stop worrying about possible disasters, obstacles, panics, or unfavourable combinations of circumstances; it is time enough to meet such things when they present themselves before you in the immediate present, and you will find that every difficulty carries with it the wherewithal for its overcoming.

Be very aware of the words you use on a day to day basis.

Words programme your brain, they invoke feelings and your feeling dictate how you feel, which dictates how you act.

Never speak of yourself, your affairs, or of anything else in a discouraged or discouraging way.

Never admit the possibility of failure, or speak in a way that infers failure as a possibility. Add the word "yet" to the end of sentences that could be negative or imply failure.

Never speak of the times as being hard, or of business conditions as being doubtful.

Times may be hard and business doubtful for those who are on the competitive plane, but they can never be so for you; you can create what you want, and you are above fear.

When others are having hard times and poor business, you will find your greatest opportunities.

"Adversity is the mother of Progress" Mahatma Gandi said.

Train yourself to think of and to look upon the world as a something which is Becoming, which is growing; and to regard bad things happening as being only that which is as yet undeveloped for good.

Always speak in terms of advancement; to do otherwise is to deny your deep knowledge of success, and to deny your deep knowledge of success, is to lose it.

Never allow yourself to feel disappointed. You may expect to have a certain thing at a certain time, and not get it at that time; and this will temporarily appear to you like failure.

But if you hold to your deep knowledge of success you will find that the failure is only fleeting and temporary.

Go on in the Certain Way, and if you do not receive that thing, you will receive something so much better that you will see that the seeming failure was really a great success.

A student of this science had set his mind on making a certain business combination – let's say a big Product Launch - which seemed to him at the time to be very desirable, and he worked for some, weeks to bring it about.

When the crucial time came, the thing failed in a perfectly inexplicable way; it was as if some unseen influence had been working secretly against him.

He was not disappointed; on the contrary, he thanked the Universe that his desire had been overruled, and went steadily on with a grateful mind.

In a few weeks an opportunity so much better came his way that he would not have continued with that product on any account; and he saw that a Universal Energy which knew more than he knew had prevented him from losing the greater good by entangling himself with the lesser initial product.

That is the way every seeming failure will work out for you, if you keep your faith, hold to your purpose, have gratitude, and do, every day, all that can be done that day, doing each separate act in a successful manner.

When you apparently fail, it is because you have not asked for enough; keep on, and a larger thing then you were seeking will certainly come to you. Remember this.

You will not fail because you lack the necessary talent to do what you wish to do. If you go on as I have directed, you will develop all the talent (or an Outsourced Team) that is necessary to the doing of your work.

It is not within the scope of this book to deal with the science of cultivating talent; but it is as certain and simple as the process of getting rich.

However, do not hesitate or waver for fear that when you come to any certain place you will fail for lack of ability; keep right on, and when you come to that place, the ability will be furnished to you.

The same source of Ability which enabled the untaught President of the United States, Abraham Lincoln to do the greatest work in government ever accomplished by a single man is open to you too; you may draw upon all the mind there is for wisdom to use in meeting the responsibilities which are laid upon you. Go on in full faith that you will succeed.

Study this book. Make it your constant companion until you have mastered all the ideas contained in it.

While you are getting firmly established in this faith, you will do well to give up some recreations and pleasure (especially those that show people living in a poverty stricken way and treating each other badly as if it was normal); and to stay away from people and places where ideas conflicting with these are put forward.

Do not read pessimistic or conflicting literature, or get into arguments upon the matter. Do very little reading, outside of the writers mentioned in this book and those they recommend too.

Spend most of your leisure time in contemplating your vision, and in cultivating gratitude, and in reading this book.

It contains all you need to know of the science of getting rich; and you will find all the essentials summed up in the following chapter.

Summary

THERE are Building Blocks Of Life, some 90 chemical elements forged in the stars, from which all things are made, and a Life Force which, in its original state, permeates, penetrates, and fills the interspaces of the universe.

A thought, created in your mind, but expressed externally in words or pictures, will eventually produce the thing that is imaged by that thought.

In order to do this, we must pass from the competitive to the creative mind; otherwise we cannot be in harmony with the Universal Energy, which is always creative and never competitive in spirit.

We may come into full harmony with the Building Blocks Of Life and the Life Force by thinking about and feeling a lively and sincere gratitude for the blessings already bestowed upon him and those that are still to come.

Gratitude unites our minds with the Life Force of the Universal Energy, so that our thoughts are vibrating at the same frequency. We can remain upon the creative plane only by uniting ourselves with Universal Energy and the Life Force that flows through everything and everyone through a deep and continuous feeling of gratitude .

We must form a clear and definite mental image of the things we desire to have, to do, or to become; and we must hold this mental image in our thoughts, while being deeply grateful to Universal Energy that all our desires are granted to us.

The person who wishes to get rich must spend his leisure hours in contemplating his Vision, and in being and feeling grateful that the reality is being given to him. Too much stress cannot be laid on the importance of frequent contemplation of your Vision, coupled with an unwavering deep knowledge and feelings of happiness and gratitude.

This is the process by which the picture of your desires are given to Universal Energy, and the creative forces set in motion.

The creative energy works through the established channels of natural growth, and of the current industrial and social order. All that is included in our mental images will surely be brought to the person who follows the instructions given above, and whose deep knowledge of certain success does not waver. What you want will come to you through the routes of established trade and commerce.

In order to receive your own desires when they shall come to you, you must be active; and this activity can only consist in more than filling your present place in the Universe.

You must keep in mind your vision to get rich through the creation of the reality of your mental images.

And you must do, every day, all that can be done that day, taking care to do each act in a successful and efficient manner.

You must give to everyone a use value in excess of the cash value they receive, so that each transaction makes for more abundance for all; and you must constantly hold in your head the Advancing Thought that the impression of increase and abundance will be communicated to everyone with whom you come into contact.

If you practice the instructions above you will certainly get rich; and the riches you receive will be in exact proportion to the definiteness of your vision, the fixity of your purpose, the steadiness of your deep knowledge of success, and the depth of your gratitude.

Online Business Checklist

All you need to do, in order to create your own online business is the following steps, in pretty much this order:

- Buy a domain name at GoDaddy or Namecheap.
- Buy the best, low cost hosting at BlueHost or Liquid Web (it's always good to keep your domain & hosting separate) and BlueHost is one which I used to use, before I moved to the "Rolls Royce" of Wordpress hosting, WPEngine.
- Install a Wordpress blog on your new hosting, in one click, from the control panel in your hosting (ask Support, they'll help you do it on the spot)
- Buy a nice premium theme from somewhere like StudioPress – your site will look more professional.
- Add valuable content to your blog regularly - everything from YouTube videos to podcast content, re-purposed and leveraged, in the way I share in this free video.
- Connect up Facebook Page, Twitter & Instagram accounts and share links to your blog content on them (use Buffer)
- Create a Lead Magnet (free gift) or buy a PLR (Private Label Rights) one to use.
- You'll want to be looking at Leadpages now, to create your Optin Pages, Thank You Pages, Sales Pages and Webinar Registration pages - nothing I have ever used converts as well as Leadpages do.
- Set up a mailing list using the very sexy list host / automation software GetDrip which at only $1 a month for up to 100 leads (trounces Mailchimp as it has so many more features based on what actions people take). Both integrate with Leadpages.
- Get a pop up lightbox on your site (Leadpages and GetDrip make it easy if you use them!), or you can use the excellent OptInMonster with other mailing list hosts, then build and nurture that mailing list with great follow up emails.
- Create a low cost product of your own ($7 to $27 usually - audio or video content is quick and easy) or recommend other people's products (this is called affiliate marketing). This offer weeds out the people who are willing to buy, from those who are just seeking free stuff all the time.

- You can get a great starter training in affiliate marketing specifically here (5 free videos), from an affiliate marketing superstar called Sarah Staar - I recommend her very highly. Visit her & watch some of her free videos here **http://NicolaCairncross.com/staar-bb/**
- Create a higher ticket item product (or find one to sell as an affiliate) and offer that to the people who buy Product 1.
- Create a series of follow up emails for those who don't buy, offering them great low cost products from other people. Create a series of follow up emails for those who did buy, offering them your next product.
- Start split testing the headlines and calls to action on your own key optin and sales pages (without having to change your own web pages) using Improvely
- Share your learning, which boosts your own online income from sales - by teaching others to make money online in the way that you have. People want to learn from people they know, like and trust.

If You Think You Might Need Some Support With That...

Here's your personal invite to come and join our private Facebook Group for free.

https://www.facebook.com/groups/thescienceofgettingrichonline/

I've also included below a link to my "Perfect Online Business Plan" which is a simple step by step Blueprint for experts, authors and consultants to start taking their business online.

https://nicolacairncross.com/just-getting-started/

If you have scrolled down to find this section, please DO NOT click those links above without reading this book first. Remember it's not the tools, techniques or tactics remember, that makes the difference between success or failure online.

It's what goes on between your ears!

I want you to be able to read this book, start to dream big, take massive action and THEN get started with the practical elements of "The Science Of Getting Rich Online"

To Your Success!

With all my love
Nicola Cairncross
Shoreham By Sea
15th August 2016

www.ingramcontent.com/pod-product-compliance
Lightning Source LLC
Chambersburg PA
CBHW071753170526
45167CB00003B/1018